RAND

The Impact of Terrorism on Public Opinion, 1988 to 1989

Theodore Downes-Le Guin, Bruce Hoffman

Supported by
The Ford Foundation

Preface

The research described in this document was conducted in 1988 and 1989 as part of a study examining the impact of terrorism on the public. The survey and analysis on which the research is based were supported by a grant from The Ford Foundation and by RAND's own research funds. This document addresses one part of the research program as it was originally conceived, an examination of the relationship between terrorism and public opinion. The authors looked at the relationship on two levels. On a descriptive level, they examined how the public reacts to terrorism and terrorists and elicited its preferences for terrorist countermeasures. On a systemic level, they posited some ideas for how the data may be interpreted in the context of contemporaneous terrorist countermeasure policy. The analysis uses data from 1988 and 1989, a period of relatively intense activity for and political sensitivity to international terrorism.

Contents

Tables

Summary

Public opinion is an essential factor in the dynamics of terrorism because without public attention, "only" the victims are terrorized. The terror and outrage must spread to a much larger audience before terrorists and their causes gain maximum potential leverage. They hope to manipulate public reaction and opinion to put "target" governments in difficult positions. Given the terrorists' motives, governments must be concerned about what the public thinks and how it wants government to respond. In the United States, administrations from President Carter's forward have sometimes been pressured by public opinion to take "hawkish" actions against terrorists and terrorist groups, preemptively or in retribution.

Despite the importance of public opinion, few attempts have been made to identify empirically public perceptions of either terrorism or terrorists, to analyze how public opinion is affected by terrorist acts, or to examine in any detail what the public thinks about government handling of terrorist incidents—much less its attitudes toward specific countermeasures. In short, no one has made a systematic effort to find out what public opinion really is and what the implications are for policy.

In 1988, RAND staff developed and conducted a survey in the United States aimed at addressing these issues. The first wave of the survey was conducted in 1988, with a smaller follow up in 1989. The timing of the survey may have given the results special significance. It immediately followed a period of relatively intense terrorist activity, much of it aimed at American targets abroad. Thus, one could expect that public awareness of terrorism and of government counterterrorist measures was high and that respondents had opinions about the issues that would not be unduly affected by how the questions were asked.

The purpose of this report is to present the results of that survey and discuss their tentative implications for policy and for future research. Specifically, we seek to answer the following questions:

- What did people in the United States think about terrorism and terrorists at that time?
- What did they expect government to do and how?
- What are the implications for policy and research?

Public Attitudes Toward Terrorism and Terrorists

The survey results suggest that except during highly publicized incidents, people were not likely to identify terrorism spontaneously as one of the greatest problems facing the world or the nation. But when asked specifically how serious a problem it was, virtually all respondents rated it very high as a world problem. Respondents in the survey saw terrorism as a much greater problem in other parts of the world than here. Yet most believed that terrorism was more likely to strike within the United States in the future. Most respondents also believed that terrorism was a greater threat to global order than to themselves. However, a substantial minority were very concerned about becoming terrorist victims and had even changed travel plans.

Although people generally professed to abhor *terrorism*, the results indicate that *terrorists* have not completely "discredited" themselves: Almost half the people surveyed felt that terrorists are not "common criminals" and may have legitimate grievances, and almost two-thirds believed that they are not "cowards." This ambivalence toward terrorists has a counterpart in beliefs about the U.S. government's relationship to terrorism. A large majority believed that the government sometimes supports groups that engage in terrorism and does not tell the truth about terrorist incidents. And almost half thought that "terrorism" is a political label for the activities of groups that are U.S. enemies.

Public Opinion on U.S. Counterterrorism Policy

Despite distrust of the government, a strong majority believed that government must act—must do something, even if it is not very effective. Preferences varied widely, but in general, diplomatic solutions (like economic sanctions) were preferred over military options, and reactions to incidents (e.g., hostage rescues) were preferred over preemptive options (e.g., assassinating known terrorists). Opinion about negotiating with terrorists was mixed and highly influenced by the wording of questions. However, there was no clear endorsement of the inflexible, official non-negotiation policy of recent administrations. One of the more surprising results involved restriction of information: Although a high percentage of people believed the media made too much of terrorist incidents, less than 30 percent of respondents favored more government control over news reports of terrorist incidents.

Implications for Policy

One of the things that emerge most strongly from the responses is that public opinion on terrorism may be far more complex and less bellicose than most politicians and commentators have assumed. Eighty-five percent of the respondents thought the United States should "do something," even though they were not sanguine that any particular actions would be effective in *preventing* terrorism. But there was no overwhelming agreement with a policy or category of policies that would indicate the presence of public pressure for actions that might alienate our allies or turn world opinion against us—contrary to what commentators have often suggested. Almost two-thirds of the respondents agreed with the statement that "in combating terrorism, it is vital to operate within the law and to maintain the moral principles this country stands for."

It is consistent with this sentiment that 85 percent of respondents supported use of *economic* sanctions and would condone use of military force—after the fact—to rescue hostages and to retaliate against terrorist organizations and nations that support them. It is also consistent that support for policy options declined as they became more inflexible, morally questionable, or restrictive.

What are the policy implications of these findings? One is that blanket statements about public opinion and public pressure should be carefully examined in debating antiterrorism policy and responses to terrorist actions. Given the evident ambivalence of the survey respondents, a government claim that it is being pushed into various kinds of actions could be questioned as disingenuous, at least. The majority of survey respondents evidently would not buy—much less advance—the argument that the ends justify the means. And even though the majority believed that the media make too much of terrorist incidents, they would not condone "censoring" the press. In other words, they seem aware that terrorism would be less "effective" if the media did not report it so extensively, yet they evidently see restricting First Amendment rights as too high a price to pay. Nor would they accept violating other civil liberties to combat terrorism.

Our findings suggest that the majority of people realize what a complex problem terrorism presents. Perhaps the most fundamental caution is that instead of using public opinion as a straw man or a bugbear for policy pronouncements or antiterrorist actions, government should heed what this survey suggests: The public does not see terrorism and terrorists in simplistic (even partisan) terms, and government would do well to pay attention to the ambivalence. Rhetorical manipulation does not wash. What people are evidently ready for is more considered—and more flexible—policy and response. In contrast to the rigid "no blackmail, no concessions" policies that successive U.S. presidential administrations have embraced, at least publicly, there appears to be support for a more flexible policy in dealing with hostage episodes that would allow greater room for maneuver than in the past.

Implications for Research

The results of our survey research and analysis are clearly more provocative than conclusive in defining the relationship between public opinion and U.S. policy on terrorism. Attitude measurement in future surveys about terrorism could be improved by uniformly (a) using multiple measures of attitudes as evidence of strength of attitudes; (b) allowing nonstigmatized expression of "don't know" answers so that respondents do not generate random responses; and (c) where possible, measuring strength and centrality for each important attitude question by asking follow-up questions. These improvements would increase both the burden on respondents and the cost of administering surveys. However, the topic is underexplored and important enough to warrant such expense in order to improve the value of our data on this issue.

Acknowledgments

A number of people were instrumental in bringing this project to fruition. Marty Gahart, who was among the original group that designed the survey instrument, also did the first analysis of the data and shaped many of the ideas which follow. Rebecca Mazel created the data files and did programming for subsequent analyses; she produced and checked every number herein. Mitchell Wade helped in the initial conceptualization of this document and reviewed interim drafts. Joyce Peterson helped to restructure the document and bring it to a close. Both Konrad Kellen and Dan Relles provided extraordinarily incisive and helpful technical reviews of the document. Beverly Weidmer researched the literature and wrote annotations for the bibliography. Karen Gardela gave advice and access to information that helped us relate this document to other RAND research on terrorism. RAND's Survey Research Group—especially Julie Brown, Laural Hill, and Stella Bart—fielded the telephone survey and Carol Llewellyn and Sharon Welz provided administrative assistance. Finally, as she has so often in the past, Nikki Shacklett brought her masterful editorial skills to bear in polishing and sharpening the final draft.

1. Introduction

Public opinion is an essential factor in the dynamics of terrorism because without public attention, "only" the victims are terrorized. The terror and outrage must spread to a much larger audience before terrorists and their causes gain maximum potential leverage. Terrorists hope to manipulate public reaction and opinion to put "target" governments in difficult positions. Therefore, they seek to create and exploit fear through violence or the threat of violence in order to attain their objectives. In the words of Dr. Frederick Hacker, a psychiatrist and authority on terrorism, terrorists seek to

> frighten and, by frightening to dominate and control. They want to impress. They play to and for an audience, and solicit audience participation. Their appearances and disappearances are carefully staged and choreographed to get maximum attention. . . . Terrorists are engaged in public relations and advertising; they are in show-business.[1]

Their ultimate ends may range from publicizing their grievances to forcing a government to release members of their group or compatriots who have been imprisoned for terrorist or other criminal activities. Whatever the end, public opinion is a critical mechanism.

Given the terrorists' motives, governments must be concerned about what the public thinks and how it wants government to respond. In the United States, there has been a pervasive belief that administrations from President Carter on have sometimes been pressured by public opinion to take "hawkish" actions against terrorists and terrorist groups, preemptively or in retribution.[2] On panel shows, in news reports, in editorials, and in interviews, government officials and commentators have expressed the fear that public demand might push an administration into actions that were precipitate, ill-advised, or likely to alienate world opinion and our allies. The media are often cited as the main culprits in whipping public opinion up to this dangerous pitch.

---

[1]Frederick J. Hacker, *Crusaders, Criminals, Crazies: Terror and Terrorism in Our Time* (New York: W. W. Norton, 1976), p. xi.

[2]See, for example, the analysis by Jeffrey D. Simon, "Misunderstanding Terrorism," *Foreign Policy*, Number 67, Summer 1987, pp. 104–120.

Although terrorism's inherently symbiotic relationship with the media as the principal conduit of the terrorist "message" has been studied extensively,[3] public opinion has received relatively little scholarly attention. There is a global archive of data from public opinion surveys, and these data tell a great deal about the extent and basic characteristics of reactions to terrorist acts. They indicate very little, however, about the specific character of these reactions and what they imply for policy. In this regard, the cumulation of public opinion about terrorism functions best as a crude indicator of how successful terrorists have been at getting attention.

Few attempts have been made to measure empirically public perceptions of either terrorism or terrorists, to analyze how public opinion is affected by terrorist acts, or to examine in any detail what the public thinks about government handling of terrorist incidents—much less its attitudes toward specific countermeasures. In short, no one has made a systematic effort to find out what public opinion really is and what the implications are for policy.

In 1988, RAND staff developed and conducted a survey in this country aimed at addressing these issues. The first wave of the survey was conducted in 1988, with a smaller follow-up in 1989. The timing of the survey may give the results special significance. It immediately followed a period of relatively intense terrorist activity, much of it aimed at American targets abroad. Thus, one could expect that public awareness of terrorism and of government counterterrorist measures would be high and that respondents might have opinions about the issues that would not be unduly influenced by the survey and how its questions were asked.

The purpose of this report is to present the results of that survey and discuss their tentative implications for policy and for future research. Specifically, we seek to answer the following questions:

- What did people in the United States think about terrorism and terrorists at that time?
- What did they expect government to do and how?
- What are the implications for policy and research?

---

[3]See, for example, the seminal observations nearly two decades ago by Brian Michael Jenkins, *International Terrorism: A New Kind of Warfare* (Santa Monica, CA: RAND, P-5261, June 1974); Hacker, *Crusaders, Criminals, Crazies;* Walter Laqueur, *Terrorism* (London: Weidenfeld and Nicolson, 1977); and Paul Wilkinson, *Terrorism and the Liberal State* (London: Macmillan, 1977). For more recent analyses, see Alex P. Schmid and Janny de Graaf, *Violence as Communication* (London and Beverly Hills: Sage, 1982); Brian Michael Jenkins, *The Psychological Implications of Media-Covered Terrorism* (Santa Monica, CA: RAND, P-6627, June 1981); and Yonah Alexander and Richard Latter (eds.), *Terrorism and the Media* (New York: Brassey's, 1990).

In Section 2 we discuss the background and nature of the survey. Section 3 describes how people perceived terrorism and terrorists at the end of the 1980s and presents some demographic correlations with different kinds of reactions. Section 4 considers what people expected the government to do about terrorism and terrorists and where support for and opposition to specific measures were likely to be found. Finally, Section 5 examines what the survey results imply about future policy response to terrorism and how further research could help.

2. Background and Nature of the Study

Why Public Opinion About Terrorism Is a Research Priority

Although the volume of international terrorism has varied from year to year, one feature has been constant: America has been the favored target of terrorism abroad. Since 1968, the United States has annually headed the list of countries whose nationals and property are most frequently attacked by terrorists.[1] This phenomenon can be explained as much by the geographical scope and diversity of America's commercial interests overseas and the many U.S. military bases around the world, as by its stature as a superpower and world leader.

Despite the end of the Cold War and the ideological polarization that divided the world, the United States is likely to remain a favored target for terrorists seeking to attract attention to themselves and their causes. There are various reasons for this:

- The plethora of readily available U.S. targets abroad.
- The difficulty terrorists perceive with operating or striking targets in the United States itself.
- The symbolic value of striking any blow against U.S. "expansionism," "imperialism," or "economic exploitation."
- The unparalleled opportunities for publicity that any attack on an American target—especially one involving civilian casualties—will get from the extensive U.S. news media.
- The fact that, as the only remaining superpower, the United States will probably be blamed for more of the world's ills than before.

During the 1980s, few issues dominated the headlines as terrorism did. U.S. citizens and interests were the targets of terrorist attacks all over the world: for example, the car and truck bombings of the U.S. embassies in Beirut and Kuwait City and the Marine barracks at Beirut International Airport, the machine-gun and hand-grenade attacks at the Rome and Vienna airports, the in-flight bombing

---

[1]Followed by Israel, France, Great Britain, West Germany, the Soviet Union, Turkey, Cuba, Spain, and Iran. Source: The RAND Chronology of International Terrorism.

of Pan Am Flight 103 over Lockerbie, Scotland, and the repeated kidnappings of U.S. citizens in Lebanon. These events alarmed the American public and raised their concern. Many either canceled overseas travel plans entirely or switched from U.S. air carriers to foreign ones.[2]

Official and unofficial spokesmen talked of pressure on successive presidential administrations to retaliate against the terrorists and their state patrons—even as the efficacy of military force was debated with growing vehemence within and outside government. In response to the escalating attacks against Americans by terrorists in June 1984, Secretary of State George Schultz felt compelled to ask:

> Can we as a country—can the community of free nations—stand in a solely defensive posture and absorb the blows dealt by terrorists? I think not. From a practical standpoint, a purely passive defense does not provide enough of a deterrent to terrorism and the states that sponsor it. It is time to think long, hard, and seriously about more active means of defense—about defense through appropriate preventative or preemptive actions against terrorist groups before they strike.[3]

By the following year, as the attacks continued unabated, Secretary of Defense Caspar Weinberger was driven to describe the hijacking of a TWA flight and the seizure of its passengers as hostages as "a war"—a view echoed in 1986 by Secretary Schultz when he averred that the United States was "pretty darn close" to declaring war on Libya.[4] As one observer noted in 1987,

> The debate over military responses is fueled by the American public's and government's growing frustration and anger toward the new enemy [i.e., the terrorists]. It also reflects the pragmatic strain in American culture that seeks straightforward solutions to the most complex problems. That there may be no solution to this one, or that solution may lie in longer-term developments beyond Washington's control, has not been addressed. Yet the continuing expectation that terrorism can be beaten raises the stakes in the conflict and places American foreign policy at further risk.[5]

---

[2]See, for example, Richard Halloran and David K. Shipler, "Terror: Americans as Targets," *The New York Times*, November 26, 1985; Ralph Blumenthal, "Many Tourists Revamping Plans in Fear of Terrorism, Experts Say," *The New York Times*, January 8, 1986; Desmond Balmer, "U.S. Tourists React to Terrorism Fear," *New York News*, March 2, 1986; Mary Davis Suro, "Fear of Terrorism: U.S. Families Abroad," *The New York Times*, April 5, 1986; Ralph Blumenthal, "Peak Season of American Travel to Europe Ends Showing Little Recovery," *The New York Times*, September 14, 1986. According to one study of terrorism's effects on tourism, the number of U.S. tourists visiting England and West Germany from June to August 1986 was 20 percent fewer than for the same period the previous year (1,794,084 compared to 1,436,194). See Chris Ryan, "Tourism, Terrorism and Violence: The Risks of Wider World Travel," *Conflict Studies 244* (London: Research Institute for the Study of Conflict and Terrorism, September 1991), p. 2.

[3]George P. Schultz, "The Challenge to the Democracies," in Benjamin Netanyahu (ed.), *Terrorism: How the West Can Win* (New York: Farrar, Straus, Giroux, 1986), p. 23.

[4]Quoted in Simon, "Misunderstanding Terrorism," p. 111.

[5]Simon, "Misunderstanding Terrorism," p. 104. See also various RAND publications from this time by Brian Michael Jenkins, including: *Terrorism: Between Prudence and Paranoia* (P-6946, December 1983); *Combatting Terrorism Becomes a War* (P-6988, May 1984); and *Should Our Arsenal Against Terrorism Include Assassination?* (P-7303, January 1987).

But how does the U.S. public really feel? How much of the purported pressure actually comes from special interest groups? And how much of it may be official posturing to justify the policy or policies that an administration wants to pursue? Because government may genuinely need to consider public opinion, because it may use putative public opinion to orchestrate response, and because the public does expect actions to reflect the will of the people, it seems very important to find out what the public does think about terrorism, terrorists, and government response. We made a start with the RAND survey.

What Are the Survey Research Issues?

Surveys are by no means the only research method for investigating the relationship between public opinion and terrorism. Done fully, public opinion research about terrorism would be set against a background of analyses of the chronology of terrorist events, of media coverage of those events (e.g., through content analysis of media reports), and of resulting government policy. These sources would represent the sequence by which terrorist acts are presented to and mediated for the public, and could shed more light on the external causes of opinion formation and shifts. Methodological work in other domains of public opinion suggests that the weakness in measuring public opinion alone is that it will be extraordinarily sensitive to external events. The timing of data collection relative to the prevalence of terrorist acts affects the salience of the topic to respondents and thus has a profound impact on responses. As Table 1 indicates, when respondents in national surveys have been asked spontaneously (that is, without mention of specific issues) what they consider the most important problems facing America, they rank terrorism well below other issues (when they rank it at all).[6] Typical of the spasmodic interest terrorism has historically attracted, this baseline awareness can be shifted by external events. In April 1986, the CBS News/New York Times Poll posed the "most important problem" question to a national sample shortly after two major terrorist incidents in which U.S. citizens were victims.[7] Terrorism was cited as the most important problem by a margin of 15 points above any other problem, domestic or international. Within less than a year, similar samples cited terrorism at the baseline of 1 or 2 percent.

---

[6]The "most important problem" question tends to focus respondents on broad political, and perhaps even domestic, issues. See Howard Schuman and Jacqueline Scott, "Problems in the Use of Survey Questions to Measure Public Opinion," *Science*, Vol. 236, 1987, pp. 957–959.

[7]Before the field period for the survey, four Americans were killed in the bombing of an airliner in Rome, and a discotheque frequented by American soldiers in West Berlin was bombed. These events preceded a period of heightened tensions in Middle East–U.S. relationships before the American air raid on Libya.

Table 1

Terrorism Rates Low as "the Most Important" U.S. Problem

	Percentage Citing as Most Important				
Problem	RAND 11/88	CBS[a] 1/89	Decima[b] 2/89	AP[c] 9/89	AP[d] 5/90
Drugs	24%	15%	18%	17%	24%
Crime	2	2	3	2	2
Terrorism	4	—	1	*	—

[a]CBS News/New York Times, N = 1533, Roper USCBSNYT.011989.R06.
[b]Decima Research Canadian-American Survey, N = 1000, Roper #USDECIMA.89CAN.R01.
[c]Associated Press/Media General, N = 1071, Roper #USAPMGEN.28-1RA01.
[d]Associated Press/Media General, N = 1143, Roper #USAPMGEN.30-3.RC3.
*Less than 0.5 percent.

This baseline lack of awareness of terrorism suggests that surveys run the risk of measuring poorly articulated opinion, sometimes referred to as "nonattitudes." Nonattitudes occur when a respondent doesn't have an opinion on the issue in question, yet offers a randomly formed response that appears well-articulated, fixed, and "real."[8] Respondents theoretically have the option to volunteer a "don't know" response, which poses no measurement confusion. For various reasons—question wording that fails to make this option explicit or the nature of the interaction between interviewer and respondent—respondents frequently would rather express some opinion, any opinion, than admit a lack of opinion.

When these randomly produced nonattitudes are confused with "true" attitudes or with ambivalence, they pose analysis problems in their shifting definition and mimicry of carefully considered beliefs. For a survey designer, the choice to use explicit "don't know" filters in questions is a function of whether investigators are interested in informed opinions only, or in opinions based on related general attitudes and underlying dispositions. In the RAND survey, for instance, the "don't know" option was not explicit. Name recognition for major terrorist groups was not high (for example, 31 percent of respondents said they had heard of the JDL). Yet two of these groups—the JDL and IRA—received relatively positive evaluations. One likely explanation is that both the JDL and IRA may have a broad ethnic-religious appeal among members of the large American Jewish and Irish communities that Middle Eastern groups do not have in the United States. This combination of low recognition with strong attitudinal cues may lead to the formation of an unstable, and essentially spurious, positive evaluation for the groups.

---

[8]Philip E. Converse, "Attitudes, Nonattitudes: Continuation of a Dialog," in Edward R. Tufte (ed.), *The Quantitative Analysis of Social Problems* (Reading: Addison-Wesley, 1970).

The reinterview component of the RAND study provided an unusual opportunity to examine the stability of attitudes. The trick in defining attitudinal stability is to define how much attitude change is "real"—that is, attributable to a shift in what the respondent believes—and how much is spurious, a product of having given a poorly articulated response in the first wave of the survey. Although the two RAND surveys were conducted in a period of heightened terrorist activities, no terrorist incidents of major significance or media exposure took place during the six-month interval between them. We can thus assume that most changes in respondent attitudes about terrorism are not based on external events or on perceived proximate or political threats. Unmeasured sources of attitude stability and change are the effect of being interviewed twice on the same topic (panel consistency) and changes in the context of questions in the 1988 and 1989 questionnaires.

Overall stability between the two waves of the RAND survey is around 57 percent—about 4 in 10 responses were changed between waves. While some of the questions with the highest stability between waves appear to be very general (e.g., agreement that terrorism is a problem in the world) and thus likely to be well considered, several of the more complex questions—the possible justifications for terrorism and the possibility of increased government control over media coverage of terrorism—are highly stable as well. The more stable issues do share some traits, however: most contain information (for example, the KKK and the Middle East) that is familiar to the majority of respondents on a general level and is likely to have a strong symbolic appeal. The least stable responses, on the other hand, are less likely to be familiar or to have been presented in a consistent fashion in the media. This finding alone suggests that attitudes are rarely as fixed as we assume them to be, and it implies that methods for detecting nonattitudes are particularly important in certain subject areas.

Nature of the Study

The findings reviewed below are based on two surveys conducted by RAND's Survey Research Group in November 1988 and May 1989. RAND undertook the surveys specifically to investigate opinion about terrorism. A copy of the instrument is included as Appendix A.

Sampling

The population of interest was adults age 18 or greater living in households with working telephones in the United States. We interviewed adults from a national sample in November 1988, and we recontacted a subsample of those same individuals six months later to see how their answers had changed. Interviews were conducted over the telephone, using computer-assisted telephone interviewing. The survey sample was generated to ensure that every telephone household in the United States would have a known probability of selection—what is colloquially referred to as a representative sample.[9] In general, our sample corresponded to 1990 Bureau of the Census data on major characteristics, although respondents were negligibly more male (45 percent), black (6 percent), young (mean age = 43), and well educated (mean years = 13.6) than census data would indicate.

The 1989 survey sample was composed of a subsample of working, eligible numbers from the 1988 sampling frame. For selection into the reinterview sample, probability for telephone numbers with Jewish and highly educated respondents in 1988 was higher than for the population at large, to allow for investigation of certain hypotheses. The net reinterview sample was 404 respondents. Except where identified, all data presented below are based on the 1988 survey, which included more questions and respondents.

Data Collection

Of the 1759 eligible telephone numbers included in the sample, we completed interviews with 1102 individuals in 1988 and 404 recontacts in 1989. RAND interviewers called each sample number, screening and eliminating nonworking and nonresidential numbers. A minimum of three callbacks was made to working numbers with no answers, or to residences screened with no eligible adult available. Callbacks were scheduled to maximize variance in time of day called, and extensive call notes were recorded to aid in contacting eligible household members. Table 2 gives the final disposition of all sample numbers. The gross response rate, defined as the proportion of all numbers for which interviews were obtained, is 34 percent. The net response rate, defined as the proportion of eligible, working numbers with final dispositions in which interviews were obtained, is 63 percent.

In addition to primary data collection, for comparative purposes we used data from a variety of other surveys conducted since 1988. These data were obtained through the Roper Center, an archive of responses to American public opinion

---

[9]The sample was generated using random digit dialing (RDD), a technique developed to allow access to all working telephones, not just those with published numbers. The RDD sampling frame consists of a subset of working exchanges (three-digit prefixes) and randomly generated four-digit numbers for each exchange. The efficiency of an RDD sample is improved to the extent that nonworking and nonresidential numbers can be minimized. This is done by sampling banks of 100 numbers unequally according to the presence or absence of a residential number in that bank.

Table 2

Call Dispositions for All Sample Numbers in 1988 Survey (N = 3250)

Disposition	%	N	%	N
All sample numbers	100	3250		
Eligible numbers	54	1759		
Completed interview			63	1103
Refusal of interview			24	434
Interview not completed			6	102
Other noncompletion			7	120
Ineligible numbers			31	1021
Nonworking			71	727
Nonresidential			27	275
Other ineligibility			2	19
Eligibility never determined	14	470		
Refusal of screener			40	186
Ring no answer			35	166
Other undetermined			25	118

polls from the past several decades; the polls were conducted by survey research firms (e.g., Gallup, Harris, Roper) for or by media or media-sponsored organizations (e.g., ABC Nightly News, *The New York Times*).

Interpreting the Data

Proportions presented in this document are not equal to true population values because of sampling and nonsampling errors. Table 3 gives estimates of sampling error for different sample proportions, including a design effect to account for homogeneity of sampled banks of telephone numbers. The error estimate is calculated as

$$95\% \text{ confidence interval} = P \pm 1.96\sqrt{\frac{P * (100 - P)}{1103}}$$

where P = sample proportion.

Table 3 can be used as follows: for any proportion of interest from the following sections, sampling error can be estimated by matching the proportion of interest as closely as possible with a proportion in Table 3. Reading across Table 3 to the right column, that number represents the 95 percent confidence interval for the proportion of interest. For example, if a table in a later section indicates that 38 percent of respondents give a particular answer, the confidence interval for that

Table 3

Estimates of Sampling Error for Different Sample Proportions in 1988 Survey (N = 1103)

Proportion	Confidence interval P+
5%	1.29
10%	1.77
15%	2.11
20%	2.36
25%	2.56
30%	2.70
35%	2.81
40%	2.89
45%	2.94
50%	2.95
55%	2.94
60%	2.89
65%	2.81
70%	2.70
75%	2.56
80%	2.36
85%	2.11
90%	1.77
95%	1.29

38 percent would be estimated by the number corresponding to 40 percent in Table 3. This estimate is 2.89 percent, so the 95 percent confidence interval for 38 percent is approximately (35.6, 40.4), indicating that with our estimate of sampling error, we can be sure that the population proportion for that variable lies between roughly 36 percent and 40 percent at the 95 percent level of confidence.

3. Surveying Public Opinion on Terrorism and Terrorists

To what extent is terrorism considered a threat, what kind of a threat, and by whom? Is there blanket condemnation of terrorists and terrorism, or is the response more complex than that? How high is the U.S. government's credibility in relation to terrorism? From a political standpoint, the answers to these questions dictate how and how seriously policymakers need or are likely to take public opinion regarding terrorism. These questions were considered in the surveys of 1988 and 1989 and in the analysis of the results.

Overview of Responses and Attitudes

The results suggest that except during highly publicized incidents, people are not likely to identify terrorism spontaneously as one of the greatest problems facing the world or the nation. But when asked specifically how serious a problem it is, virtually all survey respondents rated it very high as a world problem. Quite reasonably, respondents saw terrorism as a much greater problem in other parts of the world than here. Yet most believed that terrorism would be more likely to strike within the United States in the future. Most respondents also believed that terrorism is a greater threat to the global "commonweal" than to themselves. However, a substantial minority were very concerned about becoming terrorist victims and had even changed travel plans.

Although people generally professed to abhor *terrorism*, survey results indicate that *terrorists* have not completely "discredited" themselves: Almost half the people felt that terrorists are not "common criminals" and may have legitimate grievances, and almost two-thirds believed that they are not "cowards." This ambivalence toward terrorists has a counterpart in beliefs about the U.S. government's relationship to terrorism. A large majority believed that the government sometimes supports groups that engage in terrorism and does not tell the truth about terrorist incidents. And almost half thought that "terrorism" is a political label for the activities of groups that are U.S. enemies.

Attitudes Toward Terrorism

The United States has been almost exempt from international terrorism on its own soil. This is reflected in how respondents weighted terrorism against other social issues *when not asked specifically* about terrorism. When specifically asked, however, people tended to rate it high and to be generally more concerned about its threat to society than to them personally.

Although few respondents to the RAND survey spontaneously mentioned terrorism as a problem, 98 percent of them rated it a serious problem when specifically asked about it, and two-thirds regarded terrorism as very serious. They reasonably considered terrorism a greater problem in other parts of the world than in the United States. Table 4 shows the ratings for different areas. As one would expect, the Middle East was perceived as having the most severe problem with terrorism.

Although the United States is the country most frequently targeted abroad by terrorists, it is near the bottom of the list in the number of terrorist attacks annually recorded within its own borders. For example, according to the Federal Bureau of Investigation, only five terrorist incidents occurred in the United States in 1991; seven in 1990; four in 1989; nine in 1987; and 25 in 1986. Moreover, until the 1993 bombing of New York's World Trade Center, where six persons died, no one had been killed in a terrorist incident in the United States since 1986.[1] Given the small number of domestic terrorist incidents, a surprisingly high percentage of the respondents considered terrorism within the United States as a serious problem.[2] As a proximate threat, nearly 60 percent said terrorism in the United

Table 4

Terrorism Is Perceived as More Serious in Distant Parts of the World (N = 1103)

	Percentage of Respondents		
How serious a problem is terrorism:	Very Serious	Somewhat Serious	Total
In the world?	64%	34%	98%
In the Middle East?	86	13	99
In Europe?	46	47	93
In South America?	45	46	91
In Asia?	23	53	77
Here in the United States?	12	45	57
Near where you live and work?	3	7	11

[1]Federal Bureau of Investigation, Terrorist Research and Analytical Center, Counterterrorism Section, Criminal Investigative Division, *Terrorism in the United States, 1991* (Washington, D.C., 1992).

[2]In some respects this is even more surprising given that only nine terrorist incidents were recorded in the United States in 1988 compared with 1.5 million violent crimes and only four incidents in 1989 compared with 1.6 million violent crimes. Moreover, no one was killed in any of the terrorist incidents for both years, whereas 20,680 homicides were recorded in the United States in 1988 and 21,500 in 1989. Sources: Federal Bureau of Investigation, *Terrorism in the United States, 1991* and Department of Justice, *Unified Crime Reports*, 1988 and 1989.

States is at least "somewhat serious," and 11 percent said terrorism was a serious problem near their homes and workplaces.

In addition, respondents evidently saw the growth of terrorism as a given. Nearly 90 percent said they expected the amount of terrorism in the world to increase or stay the same over the following five years; half believed that terrorism would increase in the United States.[3] The percentage who expected incidents of terrorism to increase was consistent with findings from other surveys.[4]

In line with the belief that terrorism is a serious and increasing threat, respondents did perceive some personal threat in terrorism. We asked how likely they considered their involvement in several events, all of which are low probability but in varying degrees. Respondents were only roughly correct in their estimates of relative risk: They did see their being in an automobile accident as far more likely than being a terrorist victim. However, the difference between the two probabilities implied by their responses was far smaller than the actual difference: Although 47,087 persons were killed in automobile accidents in the United States in 1988 and 45,582 during 1989, a total of 203 Americans were killed by terrorists throughout the world in 1988 (and 93 percent of them perished in a single incident—the December in-flight bombing of Pan American Airways Flight 103 over Lockerbie, Scotland). In 1989, 23 Americans were terrorist victims.[5] Nevertheless, as Table 5 shows, 14 percent of the survey respondents believed they were somewhat or very likely to be hijacked in an airplane or injured by a terrorist bomb.[6]

An interesting issue is whether these attitudes were simply based on hypothetical conjecturing or might be more deeply held. One way to explore the issue is to ask about behavior that might reflect such attitudes. As it turned out,

---

[3]In fact, in the three years since the survey was conducted, the number of international terrorist incidents declined steadily from 456 in 1988 to 388 in 1989 and 307 in 1990, before increasing to 470 incidents in 1991 as a result of the Gulf War (source: The RAND Chronology of International Terrorism). Similarly, incidents of domestic terrorism declined from nine in 1988 to four in 1989, seven in 1990, and five in 1991 (source: Federal Bureau of Investigation, *Terrorism in the United States*, 1992).

[4]For example: 46 percent expect international terrorism to get worse in the next ten years (Associated Press/Media General, September 1989); 50 percent expect international terrorism will increase by the year 2000 (Gallup Organization, November 1989); 44 percent say hijacking and terrorism in travel will increase during the next 10 years (Gallup Organization, December 1989).

[5]Viewed from another perspective, nearly as many persons were killed by dogs in the United States in 1989 (20 persons) as Americans by terrorists throughout the world that year. Sources: Federal Highway Administration, Fatal Accident Reporting System for 1988 and 1989 (Washington, D.C.); The RAND Chronology of International Terrorism; and Dr. Andrew Rowan, researcher, Tufts University Veterinary School.

[6]They believed this despite the fact that previous studies indicate that we tend to overestimate the likelihood of being the victim of low-probability events while considering ourselves immune from undersirable high-probability events.

Table 5

Perception of Odds Does Not Match Probability of Events (N = 1103)

Event	Percentage of Respondents: Very Likely	Somewhat Likely	Total	Estimated Actual Probability
Being involved in an automobile accident	28%	43%	71%	19.2/100,000/person[a]
Being involved in an airplane accident while traveling	20	27	47	1.5/100,000/aircraft hr[b]
Being a passenger on a plane that is hijacked	4	10	14	<1/100,000/traveler[c]
Being injured by a bomb left by terrorists	3	11	14	Unknown[d]

[a]Per resident population. Source: U.S. National Highway Traffic Safety Administration, 1988.

[b]Per aircraft hours flown, U.S. commercial carriers. Source: National Transportation Safety Board, 1988.

[c]Source: William Landes, "An Economic Study of U.S. Aircraft Hijacking, 1961–1976," *Journal of Law and Economics*, Vol. 21, 1978, pp. 1–31.

[d]According to the *FAA Statistical Handbook of Aviation*, there were 518 bomb threats and two explosions worldwide in 1988.

while the respondents were far from panicked by terrorism's threat to their personal safety, a substantial minority of them reported behavioral effects. About 10 percent said they had canceled a trip overseas in the past, and 30 percent said they would refuse the opportunity to travel internationally in the immediate future, due to the threat of terrorism.[7] Respondents who perceived a large personal threat from terrorism were substantially more likely to say they would refuse to travel in the future.[8]

Attitudes Toward Specific Aspects of Terrorists and Terrorism

The respondents believed terrorism was a serious problem in general, but what features of terrorism caused them to make that assessment? In other words, how do they feel about terrorist organizations, terrorists themselves, and specific qualities of terrorist acts? The respondents had little sympathy for terrorist groups, but their response to terrorists and their actions was more ambivalent.

[7]Like other measures of perceived seriousness, likelihood responses are highly influenced by external events. In an April 1986 Gallup Poll, 80 percent of respondents said they would refuse an overseas trip, reflecting that period's high level of terrorist activity.

[8]Taken together, these responses indicate that perception of personal threat may form a distinct component of attitudes toward terrorism. One indication of this comes from the fact that responses to the perceived threat and behavior questions are somewhat reliable when treated as a multi-item measure (Cronbach's alpha = 0.54; alpha represents the relationship of the square of interitem correlations between the measured threat variables to an assumed underlying factor).

Sympathy for Terrorist Groups Was Very Low

Approval for terrorists *in general* was effectively zero.[9] As Table 6 implies, most respondents also had negative feelings about specific terrorist groups. However, a small percentage of the respondents looked with some favor on particular groups: For example, 13 percent felt at least somewhat favorable toward the Jewish Defense League and 8 percent toward the Irish Republican Army. We assume that these responses came from segments of the population with relevant ethnic or religious identification.

Attitudes Toward Terrorists and Their Acts Were More Ambivalent

Although the survey suggests that most Americans abhor groups that sponsor and commit terrorist acts, there seems to be a certain public "fascination" with terrorists. According to Konrad Kellen, "people [may not] approve of terrorists any more than they approve of murderers . . . But people are clearly intrigued by them."[10] Acts of terrorism may strike an "underdog" chord that differentiates them from other violence in the public mind. Some terrorist acts—though not all—consciously exploit this quality in an attempt to win public sympathy.

Table 6

A Small Minority Is Favorably Disposed Toward Some Groups That Sponsor Terrorism (N = 1103)

	Percentage Favorable[a]		
Group	Very	Somewhat	Total
Terrorists, generally	1%	1%	2%[b]
Jewish Defense League	3	10	13
Irish Republican Army	1	7	8
Palestine Liberation Organization	1	5	6
Ku Klux Klan	1	1	2
Islamic Jihad	—	1	1

[a]Question wording: "I am going to read a list of some groups and nations that have been in the news. If you ARE familiar with the group, please tell me if you feel very favorable, somewhat favorable, neutral (neither favorable nor unfavorable), somewhat unfavorable, or very unfavorable toward that group."

[b]See footnote 9.

---

[9]In the RAND survey, 14 people (less than 2 percent) said they felt somewhat or very favorable toward terrorists. Based on comparison with subsequent responses, however, we can be reasonably sure that their expressed approval was in fact error resulting from miscomprehension or misreporting.

[10]Konrad Kellen, unpublished notes on the impact of terrorism on the public, April 1988.

The fact that terrorists sometimes identify and exploit a niche of public interest and sympathy raises the question of what mitigating qualities Americans may see in terrorism and terrorist acts. We addressed this issue by asking specific questions about such possible qualities. Table 7 shows the results.

A high percentage of the respondents evidently saw redeeming qualities in terrorists and some of their actions. Two-thirds did not believe terrorists were cowards, 49 percent believed that terrorists are not the same as common criminals, and 46 percent entertained the possibility that terrorists may have legitimate grievances. These attitudes toward terrorists and their actions strongly suggest a public ambivalence that should not be overlooked in counterterrorist policy deliberations.

Attitudes Toward the U.S. Government's Relationship to Terrorism

This ambivalence about terrorists had a counterpart in beliefs about the U.S. government's relationship to terrorism. As Table 8 indicates, the government did not have much credibility with respondents on this score. Almost three-quarters (74 percent) agreed that "the United States sometimes supports groups that engage in terrorism"—and 25 percent agreed strongly. As for trust, 69 percent did not trust the federal government to tell the truth about terrorist incidents. Further, 47 percent implied by their responses that the term "terrorism" was losing its rhetorical bite: They saw it as simply a label that our government and media apply arbitrarily to actions—depending on who commits them. If U.S. enemies commit them, it's terrorism; if friendly groups or nations do, it isn't.

Table 7

Perceptions of Legitimacy and Personal Appeal Mitigate Disapproval of Terrorism (N = 1103)

Statement	Percentage Agreeing[a]
Terrorists are not cowards	66%[b]
Terrorists are entitled to the same legal protection as other criminals	55[b]
Terrorists are not the same as common criminals	49
Terrorists may have legitimate grievances	46[b]
Terrorism is sometimes justified	34
Can respect terrorists for willingness to die for a cause	32

[a]Not all questions phrased as agree-disagree questions.
[b]Response pattern reversed for table (agree=disagree).

Table 8

Regarding Terrorism, Government Credibility Is Low (N = 1103)

Statement	Percentage Agreeing
The United States sometimes supports groups that engage in terrorism	74%
You can't trust the government in Washington to tell the truth about terrorist incidents[a]	69
Terrorism is just a label that the government and media give to action committed by groups that are our enemies. If groups that are friendly to the United States do the same thing, it's not called terrorism.	47

[a]Response pattern reversed for table (agree=disagree).

A skeptical attitude toward government is commonplace in surveys. However, in this case, mistrust is higher among better-educated people, not less-educated, reversing another commonplace finding. This may suggest that the mistrust identified here should not be dismissed as part of survey "culture."

Who Holds Which Views

Before turning to our discussion of counterterrorism policies, some readers may be interested in looking a little more closely at how attitudes about terrorism and terrorists correlate with education and other demographic characteristics.

People with more than a high school education were

- Less likely to fear becoming a terrorism victim or to change travel plans;
- More likely to believe that terrorists differ from common criminals and are not cowards;
- Less likely to trust government concerning terrorism (84 percent with more than a high school degree believed that the United States supports terrorist groups, compared with 53 percent of those with less education).

Nonwhites and self-described "liberals" were far more likely than other groups to see possible legitimacy of terrorist grievances and justification for terrorist actions. On the issue of trust, Republicans were less skeptical of government policy than Democrats were. This may reflect the fact that the surveys were taken during the Reagan-Bush years.

4. Surveying Public Opinion on U.S. Counterterrorism Policy

Given the opinions and attitudes described in the last section, what, if anything, do people expect government to do about terrorism and terrorists, where is support for and opposition to different policies likely to come from, and what do the answers mean for acceptance of government action? Results of the survey contradicted some of the perceptions about public "pressure" that have figured in the debate.

Overview of Responses and Attitudes

Despite distrust of the government, a strong majority believed that in response to terrorism, government must act—must do something even if it is not very effective. Preferences varied widely, but in general, diplomatic solutions (like economic sanctions) were preferred over military options, and reactions to incidents (e.g., hostage rescues) were preferred over preemptive options (e.g., assassinating known terrorists). Opinion about negotiating with terrorists was mixed and highly influenced by the wording of questions. However, there was no clear endorsement of the inflexible, official non-negotiation policy of recent administrations. One of the more surprising results involved restriction of information: Although a high percentage of people believed the media made too much of terrorist incidents, less than 30 percent of respondents favored more government control over news reports of terrorist incidents.

How Policies Were Rated

Respondents strongly agreed that government is responsible and must take action against terrorism. Only 25 percent of the sample agreed that there is *nothing* that the United States can do to prevent terrorism. Half agreed that the government's inability to stop terrorism is an embarrassment. And 85 percent agreed that the United States must do something to stop terrorism "even if it's not very effective . . . [N]ot doing anything makes the U.S. seem weak to the rest of the world."

Even though an overwhelming majority agreed that the government must do something, their answers did not add up to a consensus on what that something might be, and different demographic groups varied strongly on their acceptance of policies.

Acceptability of Policies

To identify policies that Americans may judge most effective in combating terrorism, we asked a series of questions about potential government countermeasures. The first question concerned approval of the U.S. government's policies regarding the American hostages then held in Lebanon. Approximately three-quarters of respondents placed some blame for the Lebanese hostage situation on those policies. In order to analyze a respondent's general policy awareness and perceptions—and to avoid *response effects* from low information levels about current events—we focused subsequent questions on hypothetical policies and incidents.

Those policy questions can be arrayed on two dimensions: the degree to which they rely on use of force, and their potential restriction of civil liberties. Table 9 presents responses to questions about possible countermeasures on these dimensions.[1] As the table suggests, respondents showed some ambivalence on both dimensions.

Of all policies, respondents approved most strongly of an option not involving force: 85 percent favored using economic sanctions against nations that support terrorism. However, they approved almost as strongly of using force to try to rescue hostages: 84 percent agreed that when hostages were taken, the United States should try to rescue them even if some were killed or injured in the process.[2] The respondents were less supportive of retaliatory attacks against terrorist organizations or nations that support them *after* incidents that our government *thinks* they may have committed (75 percent said "yes" or "sometimes").

Respondents were more equivocal about negotiating with terrorists. Non-negotiation has been the seemingly unshakable, official, antiterrorism policy of

---

[1]Considering the variety of countermeasures investigated and the variance in levels of support, the interitem correlation among variables is strong (alpha = 0.55, excluding the death-penalty item), suggesting that respondents have consistent, nonrandom patterns of policy preference.

[2]However, rescue attempts and other shows of force generally receive more approval in the abstract than when tied to specific incidents. For example, an NBC News poll conducted during the TWA hostage incident in Lebanon in June 1985 found that only 43 percent of those giving an opinion supported a rescue attempt; during the Gulf War, levels of support for hostage rescue ranged from 29 percent to 62 percent.

Table 9

Responses Show Ambivalence About Policy Options (N = 1103)

Statement	Percentage Agreeing
U.S. should use economic sanctions against nations that support terrorism	85%
In situations where hostages are taken, U.S. should try to rescue the hostages even if that meant some of them might be killed or injured in the process	84[a]
U.S. should use military force against terrorist organizations or the nations that support them *after* terrorist incidents that the U.S. thinks they have committed, even if there is a risk that civilians may be killed	75[a]
Favor the death penalty for person convicted of terrorism	70[b]
U.S. should stick to the policy of not negotiating with terrorists, even if some hostages might be killed because of it	68[a]
In combating terrorism, it is vital to operate within the law and to maintain the moral principles this country stands for	65[c]
U.S. should use military force *in advance* against terrorist organizations or nations that support them if the U.S. thinks that they are planning to attack Americans, even if there is a risk that civilians may be killed	60[a]
Justifiable to limit civil liberties in order to stop terrorism; for example, by wiretapping phones or holding people in prison without charging them with a crime	44[f]
U.S. should not negotiate with terrorist organizations to try to solve the problems they're concerned with	43[d,e]
U.S. should order the CIA to assassinate known terrorists before they can commit future terrorist acts	40[a]
Government should have more control over how news organizations report on terrorist incidents	28[g]

[a]Percentage "yes" or "sometimes."
[b]Percentage "favor."
[c]Percentage "statement best describes view."
[d]Percentage "agree strongly" or "agree somewhat."
[e]Response pattern reversed for table.
[f]Percentage "mostly justifiable," or "sometimes justifiable."
[g]Percentage "closer to opinion."

the U.S. government.[3] When asked if they agreed that the United States should "stick to the policy of not negotiating with terrorists even if some hostages might be killed because of it," 68 percent of the respondents did agree. However, when asked if they agreed that the United States "should not negotiate with terrorist organizations to try to solve the problems they're concerned with," 57 percent did not agree, and 32 percent thought the policy should be abandoned.

This apparent equivocation may result from the fact that the first question was worded positively and the second negatively. Nevertheless, the second response is consistent with an attitude toward terrorists that we identified in Section 3: 46 percent of the respondents felt that "terrorists may have legitimate grievances." Since the second question implicitly involved "grievances" and did not mention hostages, respondents might have assumed that such negotiation would be independent of particular terrorist acts, and might even be considered *preventive* policy.

Concerning the use of force, respondents were more comfortable with reactive than with preemptive actions. This is consistent with the fact that preemptive action can be considered ethically or morally questionable, and 65 percent of respondents agreed with this statement: "In combating terrorism, it is vital to operate within the law and to maintain the moral principles this country stands for."

The latter seemed to reinforce our *a priori* assumption that the least-favored antiterrorism option might be preemptive assassination of known terrorists to prevent their potential future terrorism. However, that assumption did not stand up under a direct question about the option; 40 percent of the respondents agreed with that policy: 28 across-the-board and 12 percent sometimes.[4] While this raises questions about how people define "moral principles," it is consistent with the notion of retributory justice ("just deserts"), which is a central tenet of U.S. criminal justice. Given their attitudes about the death penalty, the respondents evidently see terrorism as a heinous, capital offense: 70 percent favored "the death penalty for a person convicted of terrorism."[5]

---

[3]Unofficially, of course, the U.S. government has in fact negotiated with terrorists, such as during the Reagan Adminstration's so-called "arms for hostages" deal (popularly known as "Irangate"), in which several shipments of weapons were delivered to Iran and two of the Americans held captive in Lebanon (Father Lawrence Jenco and David Jacobsen) were freed.

[4]Other surveys with similar questions have elicited similar levels of support for assassination.

[5]Not surprisingly, attitudes about the death penalty for terrorists are largely predicted by a respondent's view on the death penalty for murder in general: among those supporting the death penalty for murder, 86 percent favored the death penalty for convicted terrorists.

This brings us to the dimension of civil liberties. As it turned out, increased government control over media reporting of terrorist incidents was at the bottom of the list of options. A majority (53 percent) of respondents had expressed a belief earlier in the interview that the media give too much coverage to terrorist incidents. Still, only 28 percent agreed that the government should exert more control over the media.

In addition to freedom of the press, we probed on a general level whether Americans would accept restrictions on civil liberties in order to fight terrorism. Interestingly, the general concept of limiting civil liberties was accepted by more respondents than was limiting freedom of the press—another case in which questions on a specific issue produce very different results than questions about the general underlying principle. Nevertheless, most respondents opposed the restriction of civil liberties in the fight against terrorism. More than half replied that it is "not justifiable" to limit civil liberties in order to stop terrorism; only 5 percent of the sample said that restrictions on civil liberties are "mostly justifiable."

Who Holds Which Views

As was true of the attitudes about terrorism and terrorists, responses to policy differed by demographic groups. Again, education correlated strongly with certain responses. The less education people had, the more likely they were to favor force, preemptive actions, and limiting civil liberties. Respondents with less than a high school education favored preemptive actions by a margin of 25 percent over those with college or graduate-level education. Less-educated respondents also approved increased government control of the media at twice the rate that college-educated respondents did.

Those views were also more likely to be shared by conservatives: Self-identified conservatives were more likely than liberals to support assassinations. Further, Republicans were more likely than Democrats to find limiting civil liberties "mostly" or "sometimes" justifiable (54 to 38 percent).

There were also race and gender differences:

- Whites were more likely than nonwhites (76 to 59 percent) to endorse economic sanctions.
- Men were more likely than women (82 to 66 percent) to approve economic sanctions.

- Men were also more likely to approve of force; for example, 46 percent of men endorsed preemptive actions, compared with 36 percent of women.
- Women were *significantly* more likely than men to support negotiation.

5. Implications for Policy and Research

Any implications we can draw from the survey results must be tempered by several considerations: First, the survey itself has some limitations, which we discussed in Section 2. Second, the Cold War is over and with it, apparently, the support that the Soviet Union and some of the former satellite states gave to terrorist groups. This may change the character of international terrorism in ways that we cannot anticipate. Third, the longstanding hostage situation in Lebanon has ended, and there has been a lull in terrorist activities. Finally, some of the world's principal state sponsors of international terrorism are currently inactive. Countries like Syria, for example, fought as part of the United Nations coalition during the 1991 Gulf War and are, like Iran as well, now currying favor with the United States and the West in order to obtain economic aid or increase trade relations. Other longstanding terrorist patrons, like Iraq, are vanquished or, like Libya, groaning under the weight of international sanctions and ostracism. Taking these factors into consideration, we believe the results are provocative and have some important implications for policy and research.

Policy Implications

One of the things that emerge most strongly from the responses is that public opinion on terrorism may be far more complex and less bellicose than most politicians and commentators have assumed. Times have certainly changed since the survey, but we might, if anything, expect people to be even less bloody-minded now. When the survey was conducted, there had been a wave of attacks on Americans and American facilities abroad, as well as on other nationals. Yet the survey found no evidence of a groundswell to combat terrorism "at any cost."

Granted, 98 percent thought that terrorism is a serious world problem—but largely because it threatened the global community. Further, 85 percent of the respondents thought the United States should "do something," even though they were not sanguine that any particular actions would be effective in *preventing* terrorism. But there was no overwhelming agreement with a policy or category of policies that would represent public pressure for actions that might alienate our allies or turn world opinion against us—as commentators have often suggested. Almost two-thirds of the respondents agreed with the statement that "in combating terrorism, it is vital to operate within the law and to maintain the moral principles this country stands for."

It is consistent with this sentiment that 85 percent of respondents supported use of *economic* sanctions and would condone use of military force—after the fact—to rescue hostages and to retaliate against terrorist organizations and nations that support them. It is also consistent that support for policy declined as the options become more inflexible, morally questionable, or restrictive:

- A significant minority disagreed with the U.S. policy of not negotiating during a hostage incident. Further, the majority evidently favored possible negotiation with terrorist organizations about their *grievances*—a sentiment consistent with the fact that almost half the respondents were willing to concede that terrorists might have legitimate grievances.
- A government policy for assassinating known terrorists to "prevent" future acts was rejected by 60 percent of the respondents.
- Over 70 percent were against increasing government control of news about terrorist incidents.

What are the policy implications of these findings? Keeping in mind the caveats above, we believe the results do suggest a number of policy-relevant cautions.

One is that blanket statements about public opinion and public pressure should be examined carefully in debating antiterrorism policy and responses to terrorist actions. How big a role did public pressure play in government's counter-terrorist actions, such as Carter's abortive rescue attempt of the hostages in Tehran, the raid against Khadafi, mining the harbor in Nicaragua, or the alleged negotiations with Iran involving the hostages in Lebanon? Given the evident ambivalence of the survey respondents, a government claim that it is being pushed into various kinds of actions could be questioned as disingenuous at least.

The results also call into question the claim that government must do a better job of educating the public about terrorism and antiterrorist policy.[1] That claim is usually based on the assertion that the public is pushing for an extreme solution, usually involving force. In fact, our results suggest that the public might have something to teach those who make that assertion. The majority of survey respondents evidently would not buy—much less advance—the argument that the ends justify the means: Although the majority believed that the media make

[1]See, for example, Bruce Hoffman, *U.S. Policy Options to the Hostage Crisis in Lebanon* (Santa Monica, CA: RAND, P-7585, August 1989).

too much of terrorist incidents, they would not condone "censoring" the press. In other words, they seem aware that terrorism would be less "effective" if the media did not report it so extensively, yet they evidently see restricting First Amendment rights as too high a price to pay. Nor would they accept violating other civil liberties to combat terrorism. Thus, our findings suggest that the majority of people realize what a complex problem terrorism presents.

The policy of non-negotiation is one issue where government might do well to inform the public more fully. Our findings suggest that the justification for this policy is not well understood. Indeed, in contrast to the rigid "no blackmail, no concessions" policies that successive U.S. presidential administrations have embraced, at least publicly, there appears to be support for a more flexible policy in dealing with hostage episodes that would allow greater room for maneuver than in the past.

But the next question is how to inform the public with credibility. From the survey, it is clear that public trust in the government is not high when it comes to terrorism. And one fact should be especially worrisome to policy leaders: The more educated respondents were, the less likely they were to trust government on this issue. As we have pointed out, mistrust of government is almost a cliché in surveys, but it usually goes in the opposite direction: The less educated are the ones likely to distrust government. The RAND result suggests that the (potentially) more analytic and informed people are, the less credibility they give to government on this score. Richard Nixon having starkly demonstrated the problem with proving a negative, government protests that it is not deceiving the public about terrorism would certainly not be a viable start in building credibility.

It is not hard to understand why many respondents believed that "terrorist" is a label the government puts on groups that do not support U.S. interests—and that the government supports terrorists who serve U.S. ends. In the 1980s, Nicaragua and El Salvador both had insurgent groups seeking to overthrow the government. Both these insurgent groups were receiving aid from other sovereign nations. Both governments and both groups were accused of atrocities and violations of civil rights. However, U.S. government spokesmen labeled the Nicaraguan Contras "freedom fighters" and the Salvadoran FMLN "terrorists." And the flow of U.S. dollars followed the rhetoric. This is not intended to judge either group or to question policies that dictated support of the Contras. However, if our respondents' attitudes toward government are an indication, politicians would do well to consider that inflammatory language can burn both ways.

Perhaps the most fundamental caution is that instead of using "public opinion" as a straw man or a bugbear for policy pronouncements or antiterrorist actions, government should heed what this survey suggests: The public does not see terrorism and terrorists in simplistic (even partisan) terms, and government would do well to pay attention to the ambivalence. Rhetorical manipulation does not wash. What people are evidently ready for is more considered—and more flexible—policy and response.

Implications for Future Research

The results reported here are clearly more provocative than conclusive in defining the relationship between public opinion and U.S. policy on terrorism. Future research in this domain might theorize a causal model of how public opinion about terrorism is formed, focusing on the linkages between nature of the acts themselves, media presentation, and resulting public reactions. Attitude measurement in future surveys about terrorism could be improved by uniformly (a) using multiple measures of attitudes so that interitem correlation can be taken as evidence of the strength of attitudes; (b) allowing nonstigmatized expression of "don't knows," so that respondents do not generate random responses; and (c) where possible, measuring strength and centrality for each important attitude question by asking follow-up questions.[2] As always, such improvements mean an increase in respondent burden and study costs. But the price of minimizing response error when investigating such complex and unfamiliar topics as terrorism is far less than the price of its unconsidered presence in models of true attitudes.

---

[2]Tom W. Smith, "Nonattitudes: A Review and Evaluation," in Charles F. Turner and Elizabeth Martin (eds.), *Surveying Subjective Phenomena* (New York: Russell Sage, 1984), p. 221.

Appendix

A. Survey Instrument

>1< What do you think is the most important problem facing this country today? [allow 2] [loc 11/1]

===>[specify]

>2< After I read each of these statements, please tell me how likely each event is -- very likely, somewhat likely, somewhat unlikely, very unlikely, not likely at all.

Being involved in an auto accident while driving...
Do you think that is

<1> Very likely, [b]<d>[n]

<2> somewhat likely, [b]<r>[n]

<3> somewhat unlikely,

<4> very unlikely, or

<5> not likely at all?

===>

>2a< Being involved in an airplane accident while traveling...

<1> Very likely, [b]<d>[n]

<2> somewhat likely, [b]<r>[n]

<3> somewhat unlikely,

<4> very unlikely, or

<5> not likely at all?

===>

>2b< Being a passenger on an airliner that is hijacked...

<1> Very likely, [b]<d>[n]

<2> somewhat likely, [b]<r>[n]

<3> somewhat unlikely,

<4> very unlikely, or

<5> not likely at all?

===>

>2c< Being injured by a bomb left by terrorists...

<1> Very likely, [b]<d>[n]

<2> somewhat likely, [b]<r>[n]

<3> somewhat unlikely,

<4> very unlikely, or

<5> not likely at all?

===>

>3< Have you ever changed your travel plans, and decided not to take a trip overseas because of the threat of terrorism?

<1> YES

[b]<d>[n]

<2> NO

[b]<r>[n]

<9> DID NOT HAVE PLANS

===>

>4< If you had the opportunity to travel overseas this fall, would you take the trip, or would you refuse it because of the threat of terrorism?

<1> TAKE TRIP [b]<d>[n]

<2> REFUSE TO TRAVEL [b]<r>[n]

===>

>5< Over the next five years, do you think the amount of terrorism in the world will increase, decrease, or stay about the same?

<1> INCREASE [b]<d>[n]

<2> DECREASE [b]<r>[n]

<3> STAY SAME

===>

>6< Over the next five years, do you think the amount of terrorism in the United States will increase, decrease, or stay about the same?

<1> INCREASE

[b]<d>[n]

<2> DECREASE

[b]<r>[n]

<3> STAY SAME

===>

>7< Some people seem to follow what's going on in government and public affairs most of the time, whether there's an election going on or

not. Others aren't that interested. Would you say you follow what's going on in government and public affairs

<1> most of the time

[b]<d>[n]

<2> some of the time,

[b]<r>[n]

<3> only now and then,

<4> or hardly at all?

===>

>8< How much of the time do you think you can trust the government in Washington to do what is right -almost always, most of the time, or only some of the time?

<1> ALMOST ALWAYS [b]<d>[n]

<2> MOST OF THE TIME [b]<r>[n]

<3> SOME OF THE TIME

<9> NONE OF THE TIME

===>

>9< Do you think it will be best for the future of this country if we take an active part in world affairs or if we stay out of world affairs?

<1> TAKE AN ACTIVE PART [b]<d>[n]

<2> STAY OUT OF WORLD AFFAIRS [b]<r>[n]

===>

>10< Do you think we should spend less money for defense, more money, or do you think we currently spend about the right amount of money for defense?

<1> LESS

[b]<d>[n]

<2> MORE

[b]<r>[n]

<3> ABOUT RIGHT

<4> OTHER

===>

>11< In general, do you favor or oppose the death penalty for persons convicted of murder?

<1> FAVOR [b]<d>[n]

<2> OPPOSE [b]<r>[n]

===>

>12< I am going to read a list of some groups and nations that have been in the news. If you ARE familiar with the group, please tell me if you feel very favorable, somewhat favorable, neutral (neither favorable nor unfavorable), somewhat unfavorable, or very unfavorable toward that group. For example, how do you feel about..

Israel

<1> very favorable

[b]<d>[n]

<2> somewhat favorable

[b]<r>[n]

<3> neutral (neither favorable nor unfavorable)

<4> somewhat unfavorable

<5> very unfavorable

<9> NEVER HEARD OF

===>

>13< How do you feel about Saudi Arabia, would you say

<1> very favorable [b]<d>[n]

<2> somewhat favorable [b]<r>[n]

<3> neutral (neither favorable nor unfavorable)

<4> somewhat unfavorable

<5> very unfavorable

<9> NEVER HEARD OF

===>

>14< (How do you feel about) Iran,, would you say

<1> very favorable [b]<d>[n]

<2> somewhat favorable [b]<r>[n]

<3> neutral (neither favorable nor unfavorable)

<4> somewhat unfavorable

<5> very unfavorable

<9> NEVER HEARD OF

===>

>15< And what about Terrorists,

<1> very favorable [b]<d>[n]

<2> somewhat favorable [b]<r>[n]

<3> neutral (neither favorable nor unfavorable)

<4> somewhat unfavorable

<5> very unfavorable

<9> NEVER HEARD OF

===>

>16< What about the Irish Republican Army (IRA)

<1> very favorable

<2> somewhat favorable [b]<d>[n]

<3> neutral (neither favorable nor unfavorable) [b]<r>[n]

<4> somewhat unfavorable

<5> very unfavorable

<9> NEVER HEARD OF

===>

>17< And the Palestine Liberation Organization (PLO)

<1> very favorable

[b]<d>[n]

<2> somewhat favorable

[b]<r>[n]

<3> neutral (neither favorable nor unfavorable)

<4> somewhat unfavorable

<5> very unfavorable

<9> NEVER HEARD OF

===>

>18< What about the Ku Klux Klan (KKK)

<1> very favorable [b]<d>[n]

<2> somewhat favorable [b]<r>[n]

<3> neutral (neither favorable nor unfavorable)

<4> somewhat unfavorable

<5> very unfavorable

<9> NEVER HEARD OF

===>

>19< And the Islamic Jihad

[b]<d>[n]

[b]<r>[n]

<1> very favorable

<2> somewhat favorable

<3> neutral (neither favorable nor unfavorable)

<4> somewhat unfavorable

<5> very unfavorable

<9> NEVER HEARD OF

===>

>20< And what about the Jewish Defense League (JDL)

[b]<d>[n]

[b]<r>[n]

<1> very favorable

<2> somewhat favorable

<3> neutral (neither favorable nor unfavorable)

<4> somewhat unfavorable

<5> very unfavorable?

<9> NEVER HEARD OF

===>

>21< Now, I'm going to ask you some questions about the problem of terrorism.

How serious a problem do you think terrorism is in the world

[b]<d>[n]

[b]<r>[n]

<1> very serious,

<2> somewhat serious,

<3> hardly serious,

<4> or not serious at all?

===>

>22< How serious a problem is terrorism in Europe. Would you say

[b]<d>[n]

[b]<r>[n]

<1> very serious,

<2> somewhat serious,

<3> hardly serious,

<4> or not serious at all?

===>

>23< How serious a problem is terrorism in South America?

<1> very serious,

<2> somewhat serious, [b]<d>[n]

<3> hardly serious, [b]<r>[n]

<4> or not serious at all?

===>

>24< How serious a problem is terrorism in ...the Middle East

<1> very serious,

<2> somewhat serious, [b]<d>[n]

<3> hardly serious, [b]<r>[n]

<4> or not serious at all?

===>

>25< How serious a problem is terrorism in ...Asia

<1> very serious,

<2> somewhat serious, [b]<d>[n]

<3> hardly serious, [b]<r>[n]

<4> or not serious at all?

===>

>26< How serious a problem is terrorism here in the United States.

<1> very serious, [b]<d>[n]

<2> somewhat serious, [b]<r>[n]

<3> hardly serious,

<4> or not serious at all?

===>

>27< How serious a problem is terrorism ...near where you live and work.

<1> very serious,

<2> somewhat serious, [b]<d>[n]

<3> hardly serious, [b]<r>[n]

<4> or not serious at all?

===>

>28< How serious a threat is terrorism to the national interests of the United States - very serious, somewhat serious, hardly serious, or not serious at all?

<1> very serious, [b]<d>[n]

<2> somewhat serious, [b]<r>[n]

<3> hardly serious,

<4> or not serious at all?

===>

>29< How serious a threat is terrorism to world peace....

<1> very serious, [b]<d>[n]

<2> somewhat serious, [b]<r>[n]

<3> hardly serious,

<4> or not serious at all?

===>

>30< People who are called terrorists by some people may be seen as freedom fighters by others. What do you think of people called terrorists? Are they always justified in what they do, sometimes justified, or never justified?

<1> ALWAYS JUSTIFIED [b]<d>[n]

<2> SOMETIMES JUSTIFIED [b]<r>[n]

<3> NEVER JUSTIFIED

===>

>31< Concerning the continuing hostage situation in Lebanon, would you place a lot of the blame, some blame, or not much of the blame... on the policies of the United States government in the Middle East?

<1> A LOT [b]<d>[n]

<2> SOME [b]<r>[n]

<3> NOT MUCH

===>

>32< As I read each of the following statements, please tell me whether you agree strongly, agree somewhat, disagree somewhat, or disagree strongly with the statement.

I don't think public officials care much what people like me think. Do you

<1> agree strongly, [b]<d>[n]

<2> agree somewhat, [b]<r>[n]

<3> disagree somewhat or

<4> disagree strongly?

===>

>33< Sometimes politics and government seem so complicated that a person like me can't really understand what's going on.

<1> agree strongly,

[b]<d>[n]

<2> agree somewhat,

[b]<r>[n]

<3> disagree somewhat or

<4> disagree strongly?

===>

>34< Terrorism is wrong because it breaks the rules of the civilized world.

<1> agree strongly, [b]<d>[n]

<2> agree somewhat, [b]<r>[n]

<3> disagree somewhat or

<4> disagree strongly?

===>

>35< You can trust the government in Washington to tell the truth about terrorist incidents.

<1> agree strongly,

[b]<d>[n]

<2> agree somewhat,

[b]<r>[n]

<3> disagree somewhat or

<4> disagree strongly?

===>

>36< The United States sometimes supports groups that engage in terrorism.

<1> agree strongly,

[b]<d>[n]

<2> agree somewhat,

[b]<r>[n]

<3> disagree somewhat or

<4> disagree strongly?

===>

>37< The inability of the United States to stop terrorism is an embarassment to this country.

<1> agree strongly,

[b]<d>[n]

<2> agree somewhat,

[b]<r>[n]

<3> disagree somewhat or

<4> disagree strongly?

===>

>38< Terrorists may have legitimate grievances, and they sometimes have no other way of getting people to listen to them.

<1> agree strongly,

[b]<d>[n]

<2> agree somewhat,

[b]<r>[n]

<3> disagree somewhat or

<4> disagree strongly?

===>

>39< Because of what they have done, terrorists are NOT entitled to the same legal protections as any other person charged with a crime.

<1> agree strongly,

[b]<d>[n]

<2> agree somewhat,

[b]<r>[n]

<3> disagree somewhat or

<4> disagree strongly?

===>

>40< Even if it's not very effective, the United States has to try to do something to stop terrorism -- not doing anything makes the U.S. seem weak to the rest of the world.

<1> agree strongly,

[b]<d>[n]

<2> agree somewhat,

[b]<r>[n]

<3> disagree somewhat or

<4> disagree strongly?

===>

>41a< Now I'd like to ask you about some terrorist incidents that have take place in the past few years.

Do you remember the 1985 hijacking of the cruise ship Achille Lauro?

<1> YES [b]<d>[n][goto 42a]

<2> NO [goto 42a] [b]<r>[n][goto 42a]

===>

>41b< Was anyone killed?

<1> YES [b]<d>[n]

<2> NO [b]<r>[n]

===>

>41c< What terrorist group did this?
[allow 20]

20 CHARACTERS OR LESS

|____________________|

===>

>41d< Were the terrorists apprehended?

<1> YES [b]<d>[n]

<2> NO [b]<r>[n]

===>

>42a< Do you remember the 1985 hijacking of TWA flight 847 to Beirut?

<1> YES [b]<d>[n][goto 43a]

<2> NO [goto 43a] [b]<r>[n][goto 43a]

===>

>42b< Was anyone killed?

<1> YES [b]<d>[n]

<2> NO [b]<r>[n]

===>

>42c< What terrorist group did this?
[allow 20]

20 CHARACTERS OR LESS

|____________________|

===>

>42d<   Were the terrorists apprehended?

<1> YES   [b]<d>[n]

<2> NO   [b]<r>[n]

===>

>43a<   Do you remember the 1984 terrorist attack on the radio talk show host in Denver, Alan Berg?

<1> YES   [b]<d>[n] [goto 44]

<2> NO [goto 44]   [b]<r>[n] [goto 44]

===>

>43b<   Was anyone killed?

<1> YES   [b]<d>[n]

<2> NO   [b]<r>[n]

===>

>43c<   What terrorist group did this?
[allow 20]

20 CHARACTERS OR LESS

|____________________|

===>

>43d<   Were the terrorists apprehended?

<1> YES   [b]<d>[n]

<2> NO   [b]<r>[n]

===>

>44<   Once again, as I read each of the following statements, please tell me whether you agree strongly, agree somewhat, disagree somewhat, or disagree strongly with the statement.

There have been so many reports about terrorism in the news media that you no longer have much of a reaction when another one happens. Do you

<1> agree strongly,   [b]<d>[n]

<2> agree somewhat,   [b]<r>[n]

<3> disagree somewhat or

<4> disagree strongly?

===>

>45< There is nothing the United States can do to prevent acts of terrorism.

<1> agree strongly, [b]<d>[n]

<2> agree somewhat, [b]<r>[n]

<3> disagree somewhat or

<4> disagree strongly?

===>

>46< Professional terrorists are sponsored and financed by radical countries such as Libya, Syria, and Iran.

<1> agree strongly,

[b]<d>[n]

<2> agree somewhat,

[b]<r>[n]

<3> disagree somewhat or

<4> disagree strongly?

===>

>47< You can respect terrorists for their belief in a cause they are prepared to die for.

<1> agree strongly,

[b]<d>[n]

<2> agree somewhat,

[b]<r>[n]

<3> disagree somewhat or

<4> disagree strongly?

===>

>48< Terrorism is just a label that the government and media give to actions committed by groups that are our enemies. If groups that are friendly to the United States do the same thing, it's not called terrorism.

<1> agree strongly, [b]<d>[n]

<2> agree somewhat, [b]<r>[n]

<3> disagree somewhat or

<4> disagree strongly?

===>

>49< Terrorists are cowards.

<1> agree strongly, [b]<d>[n]

<2> agree somewhat, [b]<r>[n]

<3> disagree somewhat or

<4> disagree strongly?

===>

>50< Terrorists are not the same as common criminals.

<1> agree strongly, [b]<d>[n]

<2> agree somewhat, [b]<r>[n]

<3> disagree somewhat or

<4> disagree strongly?

===>

>51< In order to decrease terrorism against us in the Middle East, the United States should reduce its ties to Israel.

<1> agree strongly, [b]<d>[n]

<2> agree somewhat, [b]<r>[n]

<3> disagree somewhat or

<4> disagree strongly?

===>

>52< The United States should negotiate with terrorist organizations to try to solve the problems they're concerned with.

<1> agree strongly,

[b]<d>[n]

<2> agree somewhat,

[b]<r>[n]

<3> disagree somewhat or

<4> disagree strongly?

===>

>53< In answering the next series of questions, I'd like you to think about how news organizations cover terrorist incidents like airplane hijackings and the Iranian hostage situation in 1979-1980.

First, do you think news organizations generally give these terrorist incidents too much news coverage, too little coverage, or about the right amount?

<1> TOO MUCH [b]<d>[n]

<2> TOO LITTLE   [b]<r>[n]

<3> ABOUT THE RIGHT AMOUNT

===>

>54< How likely is it that these terrorist incidents would occur even if news organizations did not give them any coverage--

<1> very likely, [b]<d>[n]

<2> fairly likely, [b]<r>[n]

<3> not too likely,

<4> or not at all likely?

===>

>55< Some people feel that the government should have more control over how news organizations report on terrorist incidents. Others feel that most decisions on how to report the story should be made by the news organizations themselves. Which comes closer to your opinion?

<1> GOVERNMENT SHOULD HAVE MORE CONTROL [b]<d>[n]

<2> NEWS ORGANIZATIONS SHOULD MAKE MOST DECISIONS [b]<r>[n]

===>

>56< Now let me ask you a question about the Middle East. In the dispute between Israel and the Palestinians, which side do you sympathize with more -- Israel or the Palestinians?

<1> ISRAEL [b]<d>[n]

<2> PALESTINIANS [b]<r>[n]

<3> BOTH

<4> NEITHER

===>

>57< Similarly, in the dispute between Great Britain and the Catholics in Northern Ireland, which side do you sympathize with more -- Great Britain or the Catholic residents of Northern Ireland?

<1> GREAT BRITAIN [b]<d>[n]

<2> CATHOLIC RESIDENTS OF NORTHERN IRELAND [b]<r>[n]

<3> BOTH

<4> NEITHER

===>

>58< Some governments have limited the civil liberties of their people to try to stop terrorism; for example, by wiretapping phones or holding people in prison without charging them with a crime. Would you say that it is mostly justifiable, it is sometimes justifiable, or it is not justifiable to limit civil liberties in order to stop terrorism?

<1> MOSTLY JUSTIFIABLE [b]<d>[n]

<2> SOMETIMES JUSTIFIABLE [b]<r>[n]

<3> NOT JUSTIFIABLE

===>

>59< Which of these two statements best describes your view:

<1> Combatting terrorism is like any war. Tough methods must be used. Some innocent victims unavoidably will be killed. OR

<2> In combatting terrorism, it is vital to operate within the law and to maintain the moral principles this country stands for.

[b]<d>[n]

<3> NEITHER

[b]<r>[n]

<4> BOTH

===>

>60< In general, do you favor or oppose the death penalty for persons convicted of terrorism?

<1> FAVOR [b]<d>[n]

<2> OPPOSE [b]<r>[n]

===>

>61< In the battle against terrorism, which of the following policies, if any, would you like to see the United States follow?

Should the U.S. stick to a policy of not negotiating with terrorists, even if some hostages might be killed because of it? (yes, no, sometimes)

<1> YES

[b]<d>[n]

<2> NO

[b]<r>[n]

<3> SOMETIMES

===>

>62< Should the U.S. use economic sanctions against nations that support terrorism?

<1> YES

[b]<d>[n]

<2> NO

[b]<r>[n]

<3> SOMETIMES

===>

>63< Should the U.S. order the CIA (Central Intelligence Agency) to assassinate known terrorists before they can commit future terrorist acts?

<1> YES [b]<d>[n]

<2> NO [b]<r>[n]

<3> SOMETIMES

===>

>64< In situations where hostages are taken, should the U.S. try to rescue the hostages even if that meant some of them might be killed or injured in the process?

<1> YES [b]<d>[n]

<2> NO [b]<r>[n]

<3> SOMETIMES

===>

>65< Should the U.S. use military force IN ADVANCE against terrorist organizations or nations that support them if the U.S. thinks they are planning to attack Americans, even if there is a risk that civilians may be killed?

<1> YES [b]<d>[n]

<2> NO [b]<r>[n]

<3> SOMETIMES

===>

>66< Should the U.S. use military force against terrorist organizations or the nations that support them AFTER terrorist incidents that the U.S. thinks they have committed, even if there is a risk that civilians may be killed?

<1> YES

[b]<d>[n]

<2> NO

[b]<r>[n]

<3> SOMETIMES

===>

```
>67<    I'd like to read a description of a hypothetical terrorist
        incident.  I'd like for you to imagine you just heard
        about this incident on the radio or TV news.  After I
        read the description, I will ask you some questions
        about how you feel about the incident.  Here's the
        description:

        <g> TO CONTINUE

    ===>
>s1< [allow 4]                    [#which version of scenario


>s1t<  [if RND1 le <2>]
         [store <s1v1> in s1]
         [goto s1v1][else]
       [if RND1 le <4>]
         [store <s1v2> in s1]
         [goto s1v2][else]
       [if RND1 le <6>]
         [store <s1v3> in s1]
         [goto s1v3][else]
       [if RND1 le <8>]
         [store <s1v4> in s1]
         [goto s1v4][else]
       [if RND1 eq <9>]
         [store <s1v5> in s1]
         [goto s1v5][else]
       [if RND1 eq <10>]
         [store <s1v6> in s1]
         [goto s1v6][else]
       [if RND1 eq <11>]
         [store <s1v7> in s1]
         [goto s1v7][else]
       [if RND1 eq <12>]
         [store <s1v8> in s1]
         [goto s1v8][else]
       [if RND1 eq <13>]
         [store <s1v9> in s1]
         [goto s1v9][else]
       [if RND1 eq <14>]
         [store <s110> in s1]
         [goto s110][else]
       [if RND1 eq <15>]
         [store <s111> in s1]
         [goto s111][else]
       [if RND1 eq <16>]
         [store <s112> in s1]
         [goto s112][else]
       [if RND1 eq <17>]
         [store <s113> in s1]
         [goto s113][else]
       [if RND1 eq <18>]
         [store <s114> in s1]
         [goto s114][else]
       [if RND1 eq <19>]
         [store <s115> in s1]
         [goto s115][else]
       [if RND1 eq <20>]
         [store <s116> in s1]
         [goto s116] [else]
       [if RND1 eq <21>]
```

```
    [store <s117> in s1]
    [goto s117][else]
  [if RND1 eq <22>]
    [store <s118> in s1]
    [goto s118][else]
  [if RND1 le <24>]
    [store <s119> in s1]
    [goto s119][else]
  [if RND1 le <26>]
    [store <s120> in s1]
    [goto s120][else]
  [if RND1 le <28>]
    [store <s121> in s1]
    [goto s121][else]
  [if RND1 le <30>]
    [store <s122> in s1]
    [goto s122]
  [endif][endif][endif][endif][endif]
  [endif][endif][endif][endif][endif]
  [endif][endif][endif][endif][endif]
  [endif][endif][endif][endif][endif]
  [endif][endif]
```

```
(WEIGHT=2)
>s1v1<
        Today, near FRANKFURT, WEST GERMANY, an AMERICAN SERVICEMAN IN
        UNIFORM was killed by the explosion of a homemade bomb.  The
        bombing was apparently a terrorist attack.  The victim, whose name
        has not been released, was leaving a MILITARY BASE where he had
        been visiting a friend.  The bomb, which was hidden in some bushes
        near the side of the road, was apparently detonated by remote
        control as the victim drove by.  Immediately after the bombing, a
        radical group based in WEST GERMANY claimed responsibility for the
        attack.


        ENTER <g> TO CONTINUE

    ===> [goto 68]
```

```
(WEIGHT=2)
>s1v2<
        Today, near FRANKFURT, WEST GERMANY, an AMERICAN BUSINESSMAN was
        killed by the explosion of a homemade bomb.  The bombing was
        apparently a terrorist attack.  The victim, whose name has not been
        released, was leaving an OFFICE COMPLEX where he had been visiting a
        friend.  The bomb, which was hidden in some bushes near the side of
        the road, was apparently detonated by remote control as the victim
        drove by.  Immediately after the bombing, a radical group based in
        WEST GERMANY claimed responsibility for the attack.
        [equiv s1v1]

        ENTER <g> TO CONTINUE

    ===> [goto 68]
```

```
(WEIGHT=2)
```

>s1v3<

Today, near FRANKFURT, WEST GERMANY, a WEST GERMAN SERVICEMAN IN UNIFORM was killed by the explosion of a homemade bomb. The bombing was apparently a terrorist attack. The victim, whose name has not been released, was leaving a MILITARY BASE where he had been visiting a friend. The bomb, which was hidden in some bushes near the side of the road, was apparently detonated by remote control as the victim drove by. Immediately after the bombing, a radical group based in WEST GERMANY claimed responsibility for the attack.
[equiv s1v1]

ENTER <g> TO CONTINUE

===> [goto 68]

(WEIGHT=2)
>s1v4<

Today, near FRANKFURT, WEST GERMANY, a WEST GERMAN BUSINESSMAN was killed by the explosion of a homemade bomb. The bombing was apparently a terrorist attack. The victim, whose name has not been released, was leaving an OFFICE COMPLEX where he had been visiting a friend. The bomb, which was hidden in some bushes near the side of the road, was apparently detonated by remote control as the victim drove by. Immediately after the bombing, a radical group based in WEST GERMANY claimed responsibility for the attack.
[equiv s1v1]

ENTER <g> TO CONTINUE

===> [goto 68]

>s1v5<

Today, near WASHINGTON, D.C., an AMERICAN SERVICEMAN IN UNIFORM was killed by the explosion of a homemade bomb. The bombing was apparently a terrorist attack. The victim, whose name has not been released, was leaving a MILITARY BASE where he had been visiting a friend. The bomb, which was hidden in some bushes near the side of the road, was apparently detonated by remote control as the victim drove by. Immediately after the bombing, a radical group based in NEW YORK CITY claimed responsibility for the attack.
[equiv s1v1]

ENTER <g> TO CONTINUE

===> [goto 68]

>s1v6<

Today, near WASHINGTON, D.C., an AMERICAN BUSINESSMAN was killed by the explosion of a homemade bomb. The bombing was apparently a terrorist attack. The victim, whose name has not been released, was leaving an OFFICE COMPLEX where he had been visiting a friend. The bomb, which was hidden in some bushes near the side of the road, was apparently detonated by remote control as the victim drove by. Immediately after the bombing, a radical group based in NEW YORK CITY claimed responsibility for the attack.
[equiv s1v1]

ENTER <g> TO CONTINUE

===> [goto 68]

>s1v7<

Today, near WASHINGTON, D.C., a WEST GERMAN SERVICEMAN IN UNIFORM was killed by the explosion of a homemade bomb. The bombing was apparently a terrorist attack. The victim, whose name has not been released, was leaving a MILITARY BASE where he had been visiting a friend. The bomb, which was hidden in some bushes near the side of the road, was apparently detonated by remote control as the victim drove by. Immediately after the bombing, a radical group based in NEW YORK CITY claimed responsibility for the attack.
[equiv s1v1]

ENTER <g> TO CONTINUE

===> [goto 68]

>s1v8<

Today, near WASHINGTON, D.C., a WEST GERMAN BUSINESSMAN was killed by the explosion of a homemade bomb. The bombing was apparently a terrorist attack. The victim, whose name has not been released, was leaving an OFFICE COMPLEX where he had been visiting a friend. The bomb, which was hidden in some bushes near the side of the road, was apparently detonated by remote control as the victim drove by. Immediately after the bombing, a radical group based in NEW YORK CITY claimed responsibility for the attack.
[equiv s1v1]

ENTER <g> TO CONTINUE

===> [goto 68]

>s1v9<

Today, near WASHINGTON, D.C., a FILIPINO SERVICEMAN IN UNIFORM was killed by the explosion of a homemade bomb. The bombing was apparently a terrorist attack. The victim, whose name has not been released, was leaving a MILITARY BASE where he had been visiting a friend. The bomb, which was hidden in some bushes near the side of the road, was apparently detonated by remote control as the victim drove by. Immediately after the bombing, a radical group based in NEW YORK CITY claimed responsibility for the attack.
[equiv s1v1]

ENTER <g> TO CONTINUE

===> [goto 68]

>s110<

Today, near WASHINGTON, D.C., a FILIPINO BUSINESSMAN was killed by the explosion of a homemade bomb. The bombing was apparently a terrorist attack. The victim, whose name has not been released, was leaving an OFFICE COMPLEX where he had been visiting a friend. The

bomb, which was hidden in some bushes near the side of the road, was apparently detonated by remote control as the victim drove by. Immediately after the bombing, a radical group based in NEW YORK CITY claimed responsibility for the attack.
[equiv s1v1]

ENTER <g> TO CONTINUE

===> [goto 68]

>s111<

Today, near WASHINGTON, D.C., an AMERICAN SERVICEMAN IN UNIFORM was killed by the explosion of a homemade bomb. The bombing was apparently a terrorist attack. The victim, whose name has not been released, was leaving a MILITARY BASE where he had been visiting a friend. The bomb, which was hidden in some bushes near the side of the road, was apparently detonated by remote control as the victim drove by. Immediately after the bombing, a radical group based in WEST GERMANY claimed responsibility for the attack.
[equiv s1v1]

ENTER <g> TO CONTINUE

===> [goto 68]

>s112<

Today, near WASHINGTON, D.C., an AMERICAN BUSINESSMAN was killed by the explosion of a homemade bomb. The bombing was apparently a terrorist attack. The victim, whose name has not been released, was leaving an OFFICE COMPLEX where he had been visiting a friend. The bomb, which was hidden in some bushes near the side of the road, was apparently detonated by remote control as the victim drove by. Immediately after the bombing, a radical group based in WEST GERMANY claimed responsibility for the attack.
[equiv s1v1]

ENTER <g> TO CONTINUE

===> [goto 68]

>s113<

Today, near WASHINGTON, D.C., a WEST GERMAN SERVICEMAN IN UNIFORM was killed by the explosion of a homemade bomb. The bombing was apparently a terrorist attack. The victim, whose name has not been released, was leaving a MILITARY BASE where he had been visiting a friend. The bomb, which was hidden in some bushes near the side of the road, was apparently detonated by remote control as the victim drove by. Immediately after the bombing, a radical group based in WEST GERMANY claimed responsibility for the attack.
[equiv s1v1]

ENTER <g> TO CONTINUE

===> [goto 68]

>s114<

Today, near WASHINGTON, D.C., a WEST GERMAN BUSINESSMAN was killed by the explosion of a homemade bomb. The bombing was apparently a terrorist attack. The victim, whose name has not been released, was leaving an OFFICE COMPLEX where he had been visiting a friend. The bomb, which was hidden in some bushes near the side of the road, was apparently detonated by remote control as the victim drove by. Immediately after the bombing, a radical group based in WEST GERMANY claimed responsibility for the attack.
[equiv slvl]

ENTER <g> TO CONTINUE

===> [goto 68]

>s115<

Today, near WASHINGTON, D.C., an AMERICAN SERVICEMAN IN UNIFORM was killed by the explosion of a homemade bomb. The bombing was apparently a terrorist attack. The victim, whose name has not been released, was leaving a MILITARY BASE where he had been visiting a friend. The bomb, which was hidden in some bushes near the side of the road, was apparently detonated by remote control as the victim drove by. Immediately after the bombing, a radical group based in THE PHILIPPINES claimed responsibility for the attack.
[equiv slvl]

ENTER <g> TO CONTINUE

===> [goto 68]

>s116<

Today, near WASHINGTON, D.C., an AMERICAN BUSINESSMAN was killed by the explosion of a homemade bomb. The bombing was apparently a terrorist attack. The victim, whose name has not been released, was leaving an OFFICE COMPLEX where he had been visiting a friend. The bomb, which was hidden in some bushes near the side of the road, was apparently detonated by remote control as the victim drove by. Immediately after the bombing, a radical group based in THE PHILIPPINES claimed responsibility for the attack.
[equiv slvl]

ENTER <g> TO CONTINUE

===> [goto 68]

>s117<

Today, near WASHINGTON, D.C., a FILIPINO SERVICEMAN IN UNIFORM was killed by the explosion of a homemade bomb. The bombing was apparently a terrorist attack. The victim, whose name has not been released, was leaving a MILITARY BASE where he had been visiting a friend. The bomb, which was hidden in some bushes near the side of the road, was apparently detonated by remote control as the victim drove by. Immediately after the bombing, a radical group based in THE PHILIPPINES claimed responsibility for the attack.
[equiv slvl]

===> [goto 68]

>s118< Today, near WASHINGTON, D.C., a FILIPINO BUSINESSMAN was killed by the explosion of a homemade bomb. The bombing was apparently a terrorist attack. The victim, whose name has not been released, was leaving an OFFICE COMPLEX where he had been visiting a friend. The bomb, which was hidden in some bushes near the side of the road, was apparently detonated by remote control as the victim drove by. Immediately after the bombing, a radical group based in THE PHILIPPINES claimed responsibility for the attack.
[equiv s1v1]

ENTER <g> TO CONTINUE

===> [goto 68]

(WEIGHT=2)
>s119< Today, near MANILA, THE PHILIPPINES, an AMERICAN SERVICEMAN IN UNIFORM was killed by the explosion of a homemade bomb. The bombing was apparently a terrorist attack. The victim, whose name has not been released, was leaving a MILITARY BASE where he had been visiting a friend. The bomb, which was hidden in some bushes near the side of the road, was apparently detonated by remote control as the victim drove by. Immediately after the bombing, a radical group based in THE PHILIPPINES claimed responsibility for the attack.
[equiv s1v1]

ENTER <g> TO CONTINUE

===> [goto 68]

(WEIGHT=2)
>s120< Today, near MANILA, THE PHILIPPINES an AMERICAN BUSINESSMAN was killed by the explosion of a homemade bomb. The bombing was apparently a terrorist attack. The victim, whose name has not been released, was leaving an OFFICE COMPLEX where he had been visiting a friend. The bomb, which was hidden in some bushes near the side of the road, was apparently detonated by remote control as the victim drove by. Immediately after the bombing, a radical group based in THE PHILIPPINES claimed responsibility for the attack.
[equiv s1v1]

ENTER <g> TO CONTINUE

===> [goto 68]

(WEIGHT=2)
>s121< Today, near MANILA, THE PHILIPPINES, a FILIPINO SERVICEMAN IN UNIFORM was killed by the explosion of a homemade bomb. The bombing was apparently a terrorist attack. The victim, whose name has not been released, was leaving a MILITARY BASE where he had been visiting a friend. The bomb, which was hidden in some bushes

near the side of the road, was apparently detonated by remote control as the victim drove by. Immediately after the bombing, a radical group based in THE PHILIPPINES claimed responsibility for the attack.
[equiv s1v1]

ENTER <g> TO CONTINUE

===> [goto 68]

(WEIGHT=2)

>s122< Today, near MANILA, THE PHILIPPINES, a FILIPINO BUSINESSMAN was killed by the explosion of a homemade bomb. The bombing was apparently a terrorist attack. The victim, whose name has not been released, was leaving an OFFICE COMPLEX where he had been visiting a friend. The bomb, which was hidden in some bushes near the side of the road, was apparently detonated by remote control as the victim drove by. Immediately after the bombing, a radical group based in THE PHILIPPINES claimed responsibility for the attack.
[equiv s1v1]

ENTER <g> TO CONTINUE

===>

>68< Now, I'd like to read you several statements about the incident. For each one please tell me whether you agree strongly, agree somewhat, disagree somewhat, or disagree strongly with the statement.

- The incident is a POLITICAL PROTEST

<1> agree strongly

[b]<d>[n]

<2> agree somewhat

[b]<r>[n]

<3> disagree somewhat

<4> disagree strongly

===>

>69< - The incident is UNFAIR

<1> agree strongly [b]<d>[n]

<2> agree somewhat [b]<r>[n]

<3> disagree somewhat

<4> disagree strongly

===>

>70< - The incident makes me feel AFRAID

<1> agree strongly

[b]<d>[n]

<2> agree somewhat

[b]<r>[n]

<3> disagree somewhat

<4> disagree strongly

===>

>71< - The incident makes me feel ANGRY

<1> agree strongly

<2> agree somewhat [b]<d>[n]

<3> disagree somewhat [b]<r>[n]

<4> disagree strongly

===>

>72< - The incident makes me feel SAD

<1> agree strongly

<2> agree somewhat [b]<d>[n]

<3> disagree somewhat [b]<r>[n]

<4> disagree strongly

===>

>73< - The incident makes me feel FRUSTRATED

<1> agree strongly

<2> agree somewhat [b]<d>[n]

<3> disagree somewhat [b]<r>[n]

<4> disagree strongly

===>

>74< Finally, if the terrorists involved in this incident were caught and convicted, are you in favor of giving them the death penalty?

<1> YES

<2> NO [b]<d>[n]

<3> IT DEPENDS [b]<r>[n]

===>

>75< Now I'd like to read you a description of a second incident. Once again, imagine that you just heard about the incident on the radio or TV news. Here's the description:

<g> TO CONTINUE

```
    ===>
>s2< [allow 4]                      [#which version of scenario


>s2t<  [if RND2 eq <1>]
         [store <s2v1> in s2]
         [goto s2v1][else]
       [if RND2 eq <2>]
         [store <s2v2> in s2]
         [goto s2v2][else]
       [if RND2 eq <3>]
         [store <s2v3> in s2]
         [goto s2v3][else]
       [if RND2 eq <4>]
         [store <s2v4> in s2]
         [goto s2v4][else]
       [if RND2 eq <5>]
         [store <s2v5> in s2]
         [goto s2v5][else]
       [if RND2 eq <6>]
         [store <s2v6> in s2]
         [goto s2v6][else]
       [if RND2 eq <7>]
         [store <s2v7> in s2]
         [goto s2v7][else]
       [if RND2 eq <8>]
         [store <s2v8> in s2]
         [goto s2v8][else]
       [if RND2 eq <9>]
         [store <s2v9> in s2]
         [goto s2v9][else]
       [if RND2 eq <10>]
         [store <s210> in s2]
         [goto s210][else]
       [if RND2 eq <11>]
         [store <s211> in s2]
         [goto s211][else]
       [if RND2 eq <12>]
         [store <s212> in s2]
         [goto s212][else]
       [if RND2 eq <13>]
         [store <s213> in s2]
         [goto s213][else]
       [if RND2 eq <14>]
         [store <s214> in s2]
         [goto s214]
       [endif][endif][endif][endif][endif]
       [endif][endif][endif][endif][endif]
       [endif][endif][endif][endif]


>s2v1<
        In Greece this week, a tour bus full of American
        tourists was seized and its 20 passengers were held hostage
        for four days in a remote area.  In a statement issued after
        the hostage-taking, the kidnappers issued a number of
        demands calling for the release of several terrorists in
        Greek jails and the publication of a political manifesto.
        As Greek national police closed in on their hideout, the
        kidnappers fled.  None of the twenty was seriously harmed.
```

ENTER <g> TO CONTINUE

===> [goto 76]

>s2v2< In Greece this week, a car containing four American tourists was seized and its passengers were held hostage for four days in a remote area. In a statement issued after the hostage-taking, the kidnappers issued a number of demands calling for the release of several terrorists in Greek jails and the publication of a political manifesto. As Greek national police closed in on their hideout, the kidnappers fled. None of the four hostages was seriously harmed.
[equiv s2v1]
ENTER <g> TO CONTINUE

===> [goto 76]

>s2v3< In Greece this week, an American tourist was kidnapped and held hostage for four days in a remote area. In a statement issued after the hostage-taking, the kidnappers issued a number of demands calling for the release of several terrorists in Greek jails and the publication of a political manifesto. As Greek national police closed in on their hideout, the kidnappers fled. The hostage was not seriously harmed.
[equiv s2v1]

ENTER <g> TO CONTINUE

===> [goto 76]

>s2v4< In Greece this week, gunmen opened fire on a tour bus full of American tourists and its 20 passengers. In a statement released after the shooting, the gunmen issued a number of demands calling for the release of several terrorists in Greek jails and the publication of a political manifesto. Later, as Greek national police closed in on their hideout, the gunmen fled. None of the twenty passengers was seriously harmed.
[equiv s2v1]

ENTER <g> TO CONTINUE

===> [goto 76]

>s2v5< In Greece this week, gunmen opened fire on a car containing four American tourists. In a statement issued after the shooting, the gunmen issued a number of demands calling for the release of several terrorists in Greek jails and the publication of a political manifesto. Later, as Greek national police closed in on their hideout, the gunmen fled. None of the four passengers of the car was seriously harmed.
[equiv s2v1]

ENTER <g> TO CONTINUE

===> [goto 76]

>s2v6< In Greece this week, gunmen opened fire on a car containing an American tourist. In a statement released after the shooting, the gunmen issued a number of demands calling for the release of several terrorists in Greek jails and the publication of a political manifesto. Later, as Greek national police closed in on their hideout, the gunmen fled. The tourist was not seriously harmed.
[equiv s2v1]

ENTER <g> TO CONTINUE

===> [goto 76]

>s2v7< In Greece this week, a tour bus full of American tourists was seized and its 20 passengers were held hostage for four days in a remote area. In a statement issued after the hostage-taking, the kidnappers issued a number of demands calling for the release of several terrorists in Greek jails and the publication of a political manifesto. As Greek national police closed in on their hideout, the kidnappers fled. When police reached the hideout, they found that one of the hostages had been killed. [equiv s2v1]

ENTER <g> TO CONTINUE

===> [goto 76]

>s2v8< In Greece this week, a car containing four American tourists was seized and its passengers were held hostage for four days in a remote area. In a statement issued after the hostage-taking, the kidnappers issued a number of demands calling for the release of several terrorists in Greek jails and the publication of a political manifesto. As Greek national police closed in on their hideout, the kidnappers fled. When police reached the hideout, they found that one of the hostages had been killed.
[equiv s2v1]

ENTER <g> TO CONTINUE

===> [goto 76]

>s2v9< In Greece this week, an American tourist was kidnapped and held hostage for four days in a remote area. In a statement issued after the hostage-taking, the kidnappers issued a number of demands calling for the release of several terrorists in Greek jails and the publication of a political manifesto. As Greek national police closed in on their hideout, the kidnappers fled. When police reached the hideout, they found that the hostage had been killed.
[equiv s2v1]

ENTER <g> TO CONTINUE

===> [goto 76]

>s210< In Greece this week, gunmen opened fire on a tour bus full of American tourists and its 20 passengers. In a

statement released after the shooting, the gunmen issued a number of demands calling for the release of several terrorists in Greek jails and the publication of a political manifesto. Later, as Greek national police closed in on their hideout, the gunmen fled. One of the tourists was killed in the shooting.
[equiv s2v1]

ENTER <g> TO CONTINUE

===> [goto 76]

>s211< In Greece this week, gunmen opened fire on a car containing four American tourists. In a statement issued after the shooting, the gunmen issued a number of demands calling for the release of several terrorists in Greek jails and the publication of a political manifesto. Later, as Greek national police closed in on their hideout, the gunmen fled. One of the tourists was killed in the shooting. [equiv s2v1]

ENTER <g> TO CONTINUE

===> [goto 76]

>s212< In Greece this week, gunmen opened fire on a car containing an American tourist. In a statement released after the shooting, the gunmen issued a number of demands calling for the release of several terrorists in Greek jails and the publication of a political manifesto. Later, as Greek national police closed in on their hideout, the gunmen fled. The tourist was killed in the shooting.
[equiv s2v1]

ENTER <g> TO CONTINUE

===> [goto 76]

>s213< In Greece this week, a car containing four American tourists was seized and its passengers were held hostage for four days in a remote area. In a statement issued after the hostage-taking, the kidnappers issued a number of demands calling for the release of several drug-smugglers held in Greek jails and the payment of a ransom. As Greek national police closed in on their hideout, the kidnappers fled. None of the four hostages was seriously harmed.
[equiv s2v1]

ENTER <g> TO CONTINUE

===> [goto 76]

>s214< In Greece this week, a car containing four American tourists was seized and its passengers were held hostage for four days in a remote area. In a statement issued after the hostage-taking, the kidnappers issued a number of demands calling for the release of several drug-smugglers held in Greek jails and the payment of a ransom. As Greek national police closed in on their hideout, the kidnappers fled. When police reached the hideout, they found that one of the hostages had been killed.
[equiv s2v1]

ENTER <g> TO CONTINUE

===>

>76< Once again, I'd like to read you several statements about the incident. For each one please tell me whether you agree strongly, agree somewhat, disagree somewhat, or disagree strongly with the statement.

- The incident is a POLITICAL PROTEST

<1> agree strongly

<2> agree somewhat

<3> disagree somewhat

<4> disagree strongly

[b]<d>[n]

[b]<r>[n]

===>

>77< - The incident is UNFAIR

<1> agree strongly

<2> agree somewhat

<3> disagree somewhat

<4> disagree strongly

[b]<d>[n]

[b]<r>[n]

===>

>78< - The incident makes me feel AFRAID

<1> agree strongly

<2> agree somewhat

<3> disagree somewhat

<4> disagree strongly

[b]<d>[n]

[b]<r>[n]

===>

>79< - The incident makes me feel ANGRY

<1> agree strongly

<2> agree somewhat

<3> disagree somewhat

<4> disagree strongly

[b]<d>[n]

[b]<r>[n]

===>

>80< - The incident makes me feel SAD

```
        <1>  agree strongly

        <2>  agree somewhat                              [b]<d>[n]

        <3>  disagree somewhat                           [b]<r>[n]

        <4>  disagree strongly

     ===>

>81<    -  The incident makes me feel FRUSTRATED

        <1>  agree strongly
                                                         [b]<d>[n]
        <2>  agree somewhat
                                                         [b]<r>[n]
        <3>  disagree somewhat

        <4>  disagree strongly

     ===>

>82<    Finally, if the terrorists involved in this incident were caught and
        convicted, are you in favor of giving them the death penalty?

        <1>  YES

        <2>  NO                                          [b]<d>[n]

        <3>  IT DEPENDS                                  [b]<r>[n]

     ===>

>tofl< [if ofl eq <1> goto 100]

>scrt<  [template <  RND1    RND2    s1    s2>]
```

>83< Now, I'd like to ask you a few questions about politics in general.

Which candidate do you favor in the November presidential election: Bush, Dukakis, or someone else?

<1> BUSH

<2> DUKAKIS

<3> SOMEONE ELSE/OTHER

<d> DON'T KNOW/UNDECIDED

<r> REFUSED

--->

>84< Are you registered to vote now?

<1> YES

<2> NO

<d> DON'T KNOW

<r> REFUSED

--->

>85< Do you plan to vote in the November election?

<1> YES

<2> NO

<d> DON'T KNOW

<r> REFUSED

--->

>86< Regardless of which candidate you happen to prefer - Bush or Dukakis-please tell me which one you think would do a better job of handling the problem of terrorism.

<1> BUSH

<2> DUKAKIS

<d> DON'T KNOW/UNDECIDED

<r> REFUSED

--->

>87< Now let me ask you a question about President Reagan. How would you rate him on... Handling the problem of terrorism -- excellent, pretty good, only fair, or poor?

<1> EXCELLENT

[b]<d>[n]

<2> PRETTY GOOD

<3> FAIR

<4> POOR

<r> REFUSED

===>

>88< When it comes to politics, some people think of themselves as liberal, middle-of-the-road, or conservative. Other people don't think of themselves in these terms. How about you? Do you usually think of yourself as liberal, middle-of-the-road, or conservative?

<1> LIBERAL [goto 89a] [b]<d>[n] [goto 89b]

<2> MIDDLE-OF-ROAD [goto 89b] [b]<r>[n] [goto 89b]

<3> CONSERVATIVE [goto 89c]

===>

>89a< Would you say you are strongly liberal or moderately liberal?

<1> STRONGLY LIBERAL
<2> MODERATELY LIBERAL
<d> DON'T KNOW
<r> REFUSED

===> [goto 90]

>89b< If you had to choose, would you say you are closer to being liberal or to being conservative?

<1> LIBERAL
<2> CONSERVATIVE
<4> NEITHER
<d> DON'T KNOW
<r> REFUSED

===> [goto 90]

>89c< Would you say you are strongly conservative or moderately conservative?

<1> STRONGLY CONSERVATIVE
<2> MODERATELY CONSERVATIVE
<d> DON'T KNOW
<r> REFUSED

===>

>90< Generally speaking, do you usually think of yourself as a Democrat, a Republican, an Independent, or something else?

<1> DEMOCRAT [goto 90a]
<2> REPUBLICAN [goto 90b]
<3> INDEPENDENT [goto 90c]
<s> OTHER [goto 91]

<d> DONT KNOW [goto 91]
<r> REFUSED [goto 91]
===>

>90a< Would you say you're a strong Democrat or a not very strong Democrat?

<1> STRONG
<2> NOT VERY STRONG
<d> DON'T KNOW
<r> REFUSED

===> [goto 91]

>90b< Would you say you're a strong Republican or a not very strong Republican?

<1> STRON
<2> NOT V RY STRONG
<d> DON' KNOW
<r> REFU D

===> [goto 9

>90c< Do you t k of yourself as closer to the Republican or Democratic Party?

<1> DEM ATIC
<2> REP ICAN
<3> NEI ER
<d> DON KNOW
<r> REF ED

===>

>91< What was your age on your last birthday?

<18-99>

<r> REFUSED

===>

>92< CODE RESPONDENT'S SEX

<1> MALE
<2> FEMALE

===>

>93< What do you consider to be your race? For example, are you:

<1> White;
<2> Black;
<3> Latino or Hispanic; [b]<d>[n]

<4> American Indian or Alaskan Native;
<5> Asian, Japanese, Chinese, Korean, Filipino, or Vietnamese; or [b]<r>[n]
<6> Something else? (What?) VERBATIM [specify]

===>

>94< What is the highest grade or year of regular school or college you ever finished and got credit for? (DO NOT READ GRADE CODES)

<0> NO FORMAL SCHOOLING

ELEMENTARY:	<1>	1ST GRADE	COLLEGE:	<13>	1 YEAR
	<2>	2ND GRADE		<14>	2 YEARS
	<3>	3RD GRADE		<15>	3 YEARS
	<4>	4TH GRADE		<16>	4 YEARS
	<5>	5TH GRADE			
	<6>	6TH GRADE	POST COLLEGE:	<17>	1 YEAR
	<7>	7TH GRADE		<18>	2 YEARS
	<8>	8TH GRADE		<19>	3 YEARS
HIGH SCHOOL:	<9>	9TH GRADE (1ST YEAR)		<20>	4 YEARS +
	<10>	10TH GRADE (2ND YEAR)			
	<11>	11TH GRADE (3RD YEAR)		<d>	DON'T KNOW
	<12>	12TH GRADE (4TH YEAR)		<r>	REFUSED

===>

>95< What is ; ur religious preference? Is it Protestant, Catholic, Jewish, me other religion, or no religion?

<1> PRO' STANT
<2> CAT: LIC
<3> JEW H [b]<d>[n]
<s> OTH:
<0> NON: [b]<r>[n]

===>

>96< What is your zip code? [allow 10]

===>

>99< How many different phone numbers do you have in your household?

<1-8> [b]<d>[n]
[b]<r>[n]

===>[goto T700]

B. Annotated Bibliography

Achen, Christopher H. (1975). "Mass Political Attitudes and the Survey Response." *American Political Science Review*, Vol. 69, pp. 1218–1231.

"Air Terrorism: Hot Air, Cold Fear." *Economist*, Vol. 315, No. 1, 1990, p. 29. Commentary on the Lockerbie Commission's report on Airline Security and Terrorism.

Alexander, Yonah (1978). "Terrorism, the Media, and the Police." *Journal of International Affairs*, Vol. 32, No. 1, pp. 101–113. The author analyzes the relationship between terrorism, the media, and the police and the impact that media coverage of terrorist incidents has on public attitudes and behavior.

Alexander, Yonah, and Latter, Richard (eds.) (1977). "Terrorism and the Media in the Middle East." In *Terrorism: Interdisciplinary Perspectives*. New York: The John Jay Press, 1977, pp. 166–206. In this paper the authors analyze the utilization and the manipulation of the mass media in the Middle East and the impact that Arab media have had in raising the level of awareness of the Palestinian problem in that region and in legitimating the Palestinian cause.

Alexander, Yonah, and Latter, Richard (1990). *Terrorism and the Media: Dilemmas for Government, Journalists and the Public*. New York: Brassey's (U.S.), Inc. This book is the compilation and conclusions of the Wilton Park Conference on Terrorism and the Media held in January 1988, which brought together terrorism and counterterrorism experts from government, the private sector, academia, and the media, as well as victims of terrorism to discuss the relationship between government and security forces, the media, and terrorism. The principal focus of this conference was on how to apply or maintain security measures against terrorism without destroying the credibility of the media by restraining or curtailing their ability to report on terrorist incidents. An analysis of media coverage was given from different perspectives (United Kingdom, United States, and Western Europe), problems and criticisms of past media coverage of terrorist incidents were discussed as well as refuted, and finally, some guidelines for media coverage were proposed.

Alexander, Yonah; Carlton, David; and Wilkinson, Paul (eds.) (1979). *Terrorism: Theory and Practice*. Boulder, CO. This book is devoted to a multidisciplinary analysis of the phenomena of terrorism and relates the theory and practice of terrorism to wider changes in social behavior, attitudes, and conditions, and to advances in scientific knowledge and technology. The first three parts of the book survey theories and causes of terrorism, part four presents current issues regarding terrorism (hostage negotiations, terrorism and the media), and part five considers future trends in terrorism and political violence and the policy implications involved.

Balmer, Desmond. "U.S. Tourists React to Terrorism Fear." *New York News*, March 2, 1986.

Bassiouni, Cherif M. (1975). *International Terrorism and Political Crimes*. Springfield, Illinois: Charles C. Thomas. This volume is a compilation of papers presented at the Third International Symposium sponsored by the International Institute for Advanced Criminal Sciences. These include papers on various questions relating to terrorism as well as a set of conclusions and recommendations that was drafted at the symposium's end. Some of the topics covered are perspectives on the origins and causes of terrorism, the problem of defining terrorism, legal issues regarding terrorism, and terrorism and the mass media.

Bell, Bowyer J. (1978). *A Time of Terror*. New York: Basic Books, Inc. An analysis of the ways different nations threatened by terrorism have responded to such threats, the problems with these responses, and some suggestions for an appropriate response to terrorism.

Bem, Darryl J. (1972). "Self-Perception Theory." In L. Berkowitz (ed.), *Advances in Experimental Social Psychology*, Vol. 6. New York: Academic Press.

Bishop, George D.; Hamilton, David L.; and McConahay, John B. (1980). "Attitudes and Nonattitudes in Belief Systems of Mass Publics: A Field Study." *Journal of Social Psychology*, Vol. 110, pp. 53–64.

Bishop, George F.; Oldendick, Robert W.; Tuchfarber, Alfred J.; and Bennett, Stephen E. (1980). "Pseudo-Opinions on Public Affairs." *Public Opinion Quarterly*, Vol. 44, No. 2, pp. 198–209.

Blumenthal, Ralph. "Many Tourists Revamping Plans in Fear of Terrorism, Experts Say," *The New York Times*, January 8, 1986.

———. "Peak Season of American Travel to Europe Ends Showing Little Recovery." *The New York Times*, September 14, 1986.

Bodenhausen, Galen V., and Wyer, Robert S., Jr. (1987). "Social Cognition and Social Reality: Information Acquisition and Use in the Laboratory and the Real World." In Hippler, Schwarz, and Sudman (eds.), *Social Information Processing and Survey Methodology*. Berlin: Springer-Verlag.

Bremner, Donald. "Media Given Mixed Reviews on Terrorism." *Los Angeles Times*, Home Edition, Sec. 1, p. 1, September 26, 1986.

Cline, Ray S., and Alexander, Yonah (1986). *Terrorism As State Sponsored Covert Warfare*. Fairfax, Virginia: Hero Books. This book is based on a study on state-sponsored terrorism prepared for the Department of the Army. The book's main components are a formulation of a precise definition of terrorist activity by sovereign states, a presentation of "examples" of such sponsorship, and finally an identification of the kind of responses and policy that the U.S. government and military forces can legitimately take both at home and abroad.

Converse, Philip E. (1964). "The Nature of Belief Systems in Mass Publics." In D. E. Apter (ed.), *Ideology and Discontent.* New York: Free Press of Glencoe.

———, (1970). "Attitudes and Nonattitudes: Continuation of a Dialog." In Edward R. Tufte (ed.), *The Quantitative Analysis of Social Problems.* Reading: Addison-Wesley.

———, (1974). "Comment: The Status of Nonattitudes." *American Political Science Review*, Vol. 68, pp. 650–666.

Cooper, H.H.A. (1976). "Terrorism and the Media." *Chitty's Law Journal*, Vol. 24, No. 7, pp. 226–232. This paper attempts to analyze the relationship between the media and terrorism and explores the difference between propagandizing of terrorism as opposed to straightforward reporting. The author argues that while in the past the media has been a contributor to the problem of terrorism, in the future it can contribute to the solution by defining qualitative and quantitative guidelines for the reporting of terrorist incidents.

———, (1977). "Terrorism and the Media." In Alexander and Latter (eds.), *Terrorism: Interdisciplinary Perspectives.* New York: The John Jay Press, pp. 141–156. Cooper analyzes the relationship between terrorism and the media and argues that the media have often been guilty of propagandizing terrorist incidents rather than relying on the inherent drama of the incident in their reporting. He concludes that the media could be of help in the containment of terrorism if they saw themselves as part of the solution instead of becoming part of the problem.

———, (1978). "Terrorism: The Problem of the Problem of Definition." *Chitty's Law Journal,* Vol. 26, pp. 105–108. The focus of this paper is on the problem of definition and what is meant by definition rather than on the definition itself. While the author does not attempt to suggest a definition of terrorism, he does explore some of the difficulties of the definitional process.

Cooper, Joel, and Croyle, Robert T. (1984). "Attitudes and Attitude Change." *Annual Review of Psychology*, Vol. 35, pp. 395–426.

Cordes, Bonnie; Jenkins, Brian M.; Kellen, Konrad; et al. (June 1985). *A Conceptual Framework for Analyzing Terrorist Groups.* Santa Monica, CA: RAND, R-3151. Describes an analytical framework developed at RAND for studying the characteristics of terrorists.

DeBoer, Connie (1979). "The Polls: Terrorism and Hijacking." *Public Opinion Quarterly*, Vol. 43, No. 9, p. 410. Lists results for a number of items taken from public opinion surveys conducted by several different research institutions on the subject of terrorism.

Department of Justice, *Unified Crime Reports*, 1988 and 1989.

Eiser, Richard J. (1986). *Social Psychology: Attitudes, Cognition and Social Behavior.* Cambridge: Cambridge University Press.

Faulkenberry, G. David, and Mason, Robert (1980). "Characteristics of Nonopinion and No Opinion Response Groups." *Public Opinion Quarterly*, Vol. 42, pp. 533–543.

———, "Fear of Terrorism Runs Wide, Deep." *USA Today*, January 19, 1991, p. 9.

Federal Bureau of Investigation, Terrorist Research and Analytical Center, Counterterrorism Section, Criminal Investigative Division, *Terrorism in the United States, 1990*, Washington, D.C., 1991.

Federal Highway Administration, Fatal Accident Reporting System, 1988 and 1989.

Grant, Lawrence V., and Patterson, John W. (1975). "Nonattitudes: The Measurement Problem and Its Consequences." *Political Methodology*, Vol. 2, pp. 455–475.

Greisman, H. C. (1977). "Social Meaning of Terrorism: Reification, Violence, and Social Control." *Contemporary Crises*, Vol. 1, pp. 303–318. This paper approaches the act of terrorism as the result of the assignment of social meanings which impute either legitimacy or outrage to the behavior. The author explores the process of reification, particularly in the arena of terrorist acts, and attempts to explain the paradox of why state or official terrorism is perceived as legitimate while nonstate terrorism is perceived as evil.

Groves, Robert M. (1989). *Survey Costs and Errors*. New York: Wiley and Sons.

Hacker, Frederick J. (1976). *Crusaders, Criminals, Crazies: Terror and Terrorism in Our Time*. New York: W. W. Norton.

Halloran, Richard, and Shipler, David K. "Terror: Americans as Targets." *The New York Times*, November 26, 1985.

Herman, Edward S. (1982). *The Real Terror Network: Terrorism in Fact and Propaganda*. Boston: South End Press. This book attempts to show the "real terror network," the U.S.-sponsored authoritarian states, and examines the way in which the Western media have managed to keep this out of the public's eye by covering only those terrorists who pose a threat to Western interests.

Heyman, Edward, and Mickolus, Edward (1980). "Comment: Observations on 'Why Violence Spreads.'" *International Studies Quarterly*, Vol. 24, No. 2, pp. 299–305.

Hoffman, Bruce (August 1989). *U.S. Policy Options to the Hostage Crisis in Lebanon*. Santa Monica, CA: RAND, P-7585.

Hovland, Carl (1959). "Reconciling Conflicting Results Derived from Experimental and Survey Studies of Attitude Change." *The American Psychologist*, Vol. 14, pp. 8–17.

Iyengar, Shanto (1989). "How Citizens Think About National Issues: A Matter of Responsibility." *American Journal of Political Science*, Vol. 33, No. 4, pp. 878–900. A domain-specific model of public opinions is proposed in which attribution of issue responsibility is a significant determinant of individuals' issue opinions and attitudes. Two dimensions of issue responsibility are assessed: causal responsibility focuses on the origins of the issue, while treatment responsibility focuses on alleviation of the issue. The model is tested with a sample of four issues: poverty, racial inequality, crime, and terrorism. The results indicate that for all four issues, attributions of responsibility significantly affect issue opinions independently of partisanship, liberal-conservative orientation, information, and socioeconomic status. In general, agents of causal responsibility are viewed negatively while agents of treatment responsibility are viewed positively. In conclusion, the importance of domain-specificity for public opinion research is considered.

Jenkins, Brian Michael (June 1974). *International Terrorism: A New Kind of Warfare.* Santa Monica, CA: RAND, P-5261.

———, (June 1979). *The Terrorist Mindset and Terrorist Decisionmaking: Two Areas of Ignorance.* Santa Monica, CA: RAND, P-6340. This paper identifies two areas of ignorance in the current study of the phenomenon of terrorism: how terrorists think, and how terrorist groups make their decisions.

———, (May 1980). *Terrorism In the United States.* Santa Monica, CA: RAND, P-6474. The author briefly analyzes terrorism in the United States and concludes that while the United States has not been immune to terrorist violence, there is a general perception to the contrary, largely because the United States has been immune to spectacular acts of political violence. He also posits that the high level of violent crime in the United States overshadows the comparatively low level of political violence. He sums up by saying that while there does not appear to be a major threat of terrorism in the United States at the present time, controversial issues such as abortion and nuclear power or events abroad may inspire domestic campaigns of terrorism.

———, (December 1980). *Terrorism in the 1980s.* Santa Monica, CA: RAND, P-6564. The author analyzes terrorist trends in the 1980s and concludes that while terrorist activity is on the rise, terrorists are at a juncture in which they are facing diminishing returns and a downhill slope in publicity. In light of this, terrorists might change their tactics and targets, which could alternately lead to greater disruption but not necessarily greater casualties or to higher orders of violence. He also concludes that political violence in the United States in the near future will not be indigenous, but will rather mirror developments abroad.

———, (February 1981). *Fighting Terrorism: An Enduring Task.* Santa Monica, CA: RAND, P-6585. An interview with the Italian News Service ADN-Kronos, in which several different aspects of terrorism are discussed including the role of the media in dealing with terrorism.

———, (June 1981). *The Psychological Implications of Media-Covered Terrorism.* Santa Monica, CA: RAND, P-6627. The author looks at the relationship between the media and terrorists, posits some of the problems in this relationship, and cautions about some of the effects that these problems are rendering.

———, (December 1982). *Terrorism and Beyond: An International Conference on Terrorism and Low-Level Conflict.* Santa Monica, CA: RAND, R-2714-DOE/DOJ/DOS/RC.

———, (June 1983). *New Modes of Conflict.* Santa Monica, CA: RAND, R-3009-DNA. A look at the types of armed conflict one can expect in the last quarter of the twentieth century. The author suggests that this will most likely be low-level conflicts in the form of guerrilla warfare and terrorism. He also explores some of the constraints on military and public opinion presented by this type of conflict.

———, (December 1983). *Terrorism: Between Prudence and Paranoia.* Santa Monica, CA: RAND, P-6946.

———, (May 1984). *Combatting Terrorism Becomes a War.* Santa Monica, CA: RAND, P-6988.

———, (January 1987). *Should Our Arsenal Against Terrorism Include Assassination?* Santa Monica, CA: RAND, P-7303.

Jenkins, Brian; Tanham, George; Wainstein, Eleanor; and Sullivan, Gerald (March 1977). *U.S. Preparation for Future Low-Level Conflict.* Santa Monica, CA: RAND, P-5830. Report of a Discussion, October 19–20, 1976, at the RAND Corporation, Washington, D.C. This paper summarizes the conclusions of a two-day discussion that took a preliminary cut at the types of threats foreseen in the United States, the U.S. forces available and needed, institutional incentives and disincentives, type of national organization required, public attitudes, and legal implications.

Johnpoll, Bernard (1977). "Terrorism and the Media in the United States." In *Terrorism: Interdisciplinary Perspectives.* New York: The John Jay Press, pp. 157–165. The author analyzes the manner in which the media have covered terrorist incidents in the United States and concludes that there is little evidence to indicate that publicity spawns terrorism and therefore that there should be no restraints on the media's coverage of terrorism.

Johnson, Chalmers (1977). "Terror." *Society*, Vol. 15, pp. 48–52. This brief paper examines some of the trends, causes, and dilemmas around the issue of contemporary terrorism, with particular attention given to the problem of how to reduce terrorism without curtailing or suspending certain civil liberties and in fact becoming an authoritarian society.

Katz, Daniel (1960). "The Functional Approach to the Study of Attitudes." *Public Opinion Quarterly*, Vol. 24. pp. 163–204.

Katz, Elihu (1980). "Conceptualizing Media Effects." *Studies in Communication*, Vol. 1, pp. 119–141. The paper reviews a succession of approaches to the study of media effects, attempting to identify the definition of effect implicit in each approach and the "balance of power" between mass media and their audiences. The author attempts to demonstrate that the "power" of the media rises and falls as a function of the importance attributed to the intervening processes of selectivity and interpersonal relations. Thus, he tries to trace the changing conceptualizations of effect in early and still-current work on persuasion, gratifications, and diffusion, and in more recent work on agenda-setting, knowledge gaps, socialization, cognitive processing of communications, and ideological formation, or "consciousness." The author also tries to show the relative power assigned to media and audience in each of these traditions of empirical work and how this power reflects changing beliefs in the effects of the media and in the possibility of achieving individual autonomy in modern society.

Katz, Elihu, and Szecsko, Tamas (1981). *Mass Media and Social Change.* Beverly Hills, CA: Sage Publications, Inc. A collection of papers presented at the 9th World Congress of Sociology, which essentially debate theory and research on mass communication and discuss the question of whether the media act as agents of change or of the status quo.

Kellen, Konrad (December 1982). *On Terrorists and Terrorism.* Santa Monica, CA: RAND, N-1942-RC. The author presents different aspects of terrorists and terrorism (aims, constituency, socioeconomic and educational patterns) in an attempt to compile information that will help predict what, where, how, and why terrorists choose their targets.

———, (November 1979). *Terrorists—What Are They Like? How Some Terrorists Describe Their World and Their Actions.* Santa Monica, CA: RAND, N-1300-SL. This report tries to convey information on what turns individuals into terrorists, how such terrorists see their world and themselves in it, and what motivates them to do what they do. It also examines what their existence is like in the terrorist fold; what problems and satisfactions they derive from their interpersonal relations; what external problems and internal anxieties they deal with; and what leads them—in the few cases where it has happened—to take the extremely difficult and hazardous step of leaving the fold.

———, (April 1988). Unpublished notes on the impact of terrorism on the public.

Kupperman, Robert, and Trent, Darrell (1979). *Terrorism: Threat, Reality, Response.* Stanford, California: Hoover Institution Press. This book is concerned more with the technological and management aspects of antiterrorism than with the general issues surrounding terrorism (definition, causes, trends).

Laqueur, Walter (1977). *Terrorism.* London: Weidenfeld and Nicolson.

Larsen, Otto (ed.) (1968). *Violence and the Mass Media.* New York: Harper & Row. This book essentially tackles the issue of the effects of the portrayal of violence in the mass media. It includes material on the individual and social effects of media violence, on the history and character of violent content in mass communication, on the methodological problems in studying these effects, on the mechanisms of local and national protest that lead to control efforts, and on the nature and impact of censorship.

Levy, Rudolf (1985). "Terrorism and the Mass Media." *Military Intelligence,* Vol. 11. Dr. Levy examines the increasing role played by the media during terrorist incidents.

Livingston, Marius H. (ed.) (1978). *International Terrorism in the Contemporary World*. Westport, Connecticut: Greenwood Press. A volume dedicated to the analysis of the phenomena of terrorism and its consequences. Contains a section on the political consequences of international terrorism, and it tackles some of the legal problems in dealing with international terrorism.

Midlarsky, Manus I.; Crenshaw, Martha; and Yoshida, Fumihiko (1980). "Why Violence Spreads: The Contagion of International Terrorism." *International Studies Quarterly*, Vol. 24, No. 2, pp. 262–298. This study examines the spread of international terrorism from 1968 to 1974. Using Poisson and negative binomial probability models, a diffusion of international terrorism was found in the first segment of the time period (1968–1971) and contagion as a direct modeling process in the second (1973–1974). Accordingly, the theory of hierarchies in which the diplomatic status of a country predicts its degree of imitability was found to operate among Latin American countries during the second portion of the overall period, but not during the first. An inverse hierarchy is suggested as an explanation for the contagion of violence from Latin America and other Third World countries to Western Europe. Auto correlation functions were used to assess which forms of terrorism were most contagious in which regions.

Miller, Abraham H. (1980). *Terrorism and Hostage Negotiations.* Boulder, CO: Westview Press. The author analyzes the problems surrounding hostage negotiations (tactical problems, transference, political climate, media intrusion) and concludes that a predetermined set of tactics is required and that a policy of complete non-negotiation does not act as a deterrent to political hostage taking and in fact can have negative consequences. The author also analyzes government policy in these situations and makes suggestions for changes in perception and training of personnel for dealing with this problem.

Nisbett, Richard E., and Wilson, Timothy DeCamp (1977). "Telling More Than We Can Know: Verbal Reports on Mental Processes." *Psychological Review*, Vol. 84, No. 3, pp. 231–259.

Norton, Augustus R., and Greenberg, Martin H. (1980). *International Terrorism: An Annotated Bibliography and Research Guide*. Boulder, CO: Westview Press.

O'Ballance, Edgar (1979). *Language of Violence: The Blood Politics of Terrorism.* San Rafael, CA: Presidio Press. Offers an overview on the history of terrorism and examples of different terrorist groups and individuals, from the Israeli Mossad to the Fedayeen and Carlos the Jackal. The author concludes that the continued success or eventual failure of terrorism depends on preventive measures and suggests that this can be done only by increased cooperation between governments and crisis management training for security forces.

Paletz, David L.; Fozzard, Peter A.; and Ayanian, John Z. (1982). "The I.R.A., the Red Brigades, and the F.A.L.N. in the New York Times." *Journal of Communication*, Vol. 32, No. 2, pp. 162–163. By studying the content of *New York Times* stories on the I.R.A., the Red Brigades, and the F.A.L.N., the authors attempt to dispute the currently popular notion that media coverage of terrorist incidents serves to legitimate terrorist groups and their causes.

Instead, they find that news coverage generally ignores the motivations, objectives, and long-term goals of violent organizations.

Picard, Robert G. (1988). "Inciting Terrorism: Are the Media Guilty As Charged?" *Security Management*, Vol. 32, No. 1, pp. 123–131. The author dissects the notion of media as contagion of terrorism and concludes that no causal link between media coverage and the spread of terrorism has been established using any acceptable social science research methods.

RAND Chronology of International Terrorism, an on-line computerized database maintained by RAND on international terrorist incidents from 1968 to the present.

Ryan, Chris (September 1991). "Tourism, Terrorism, and Violence: The Risks of Wider World Travel." *Conflict Studies 244*.

Schmid, Alex P., and de Graaf, Janny (1982). *Violence As Communication.* London and Beverly Hills: Sage.

Schultz, George P. (1986). "The Challenge to the Democracies." In Benjamin Netanyahu (ed.), *Terrorism: How the West Can Win*. New York: Farrar, Straus, Giroux.

Schuman, Howard, and Presser, Stanley (1980). "Public Opinion and Public Ignorance: The Fine Line Between Attitudes and Nonattitudes." *American Journal of Sociology*, Vol. 85, pp. 1214–1225.

Schuman, Howard, and Kalton, Graham (1985). "Survey Methods." In G. Lindzey and E. Aronson (eds.), *Handbook of Social Psychology*, Vol. I. New York: Random House.

Schuman, Howard, and Scott, Jacqueline (1987). "Problems in the Use of Survey Questions to Measure Public Opinion." *Science*, Vol. 236, pp. 957–959.

Simon, Jeffrey D. (1987). "Misunderstanding Terrorism." *Foreign Policy*, No. 67, pp. 104–120.

Smith, Tom W. (1984). "Nonattitudes: A Review and Evaluation." In Charles F. Turner and Elizabeth Martin (eds.), *Surveying Subjective Phenomena*, Vol. 2. New York: Russell Sage.

Suro, Mary Davis. "Fear of Terrorism: U.S. Families Abroad," *The New York Times*, April 5, 1986.

"Terrorist Attack in U.S. Seen Somewhat Likely." *Washington Post*, April 7, 1989, p. A17. Brief analysis of Washington Post–ABC News Poll.

Tourangeau, Roger (1984). "Cognitive Sciences and Survey Methods." In Jabine, Straf, Tanur, and Tourangeau (eds.), *Cognitive Aspects of Survey Methodology: Building a Bridge Between Disciplines*. San Francisco: Jossey-Bass.

Waksberg, Joseph (1978). "Sampling Methods for Random Digit Dialing." *Journal of the American Statistical Association*, Vol. 73, No. 361, pp. 40–46.

Weimann, Gabriel (1983). "The Theater of Terror: Effects of Press Coverage." *Journal of Communication*, Vol. 33, pp. 38–45. The author analyzes the role that the media play in image formation, attitude change, and the formation of public opinion, and he concludes that terrorists benefit from the "status conferral function" of the media, while the media benefit from the dramatic features necessary for a good story, which terrorist events provide. He posits that these speculations can serve as a hypothesis for a systematic analysis of media coverage of terrorist events and can perhaps illuminate the impact of the "theater of terror" created by the media.

——— (1987). "Conceptualizing the Effects of Mass-Mediated Terrorism." *Political Communication and Persuasion*, Vol. 4, pp. 213–216. The author attempts to conceptualize basic effects of mass-mediated terrorism by relating media-effects studies to the case of terrorism and public opinion.

Wilkinson, Paul (1977). *Terrorism and the Liberal State*. London: Macmillan.

Wilkinson, Paul (ed.) (1981). *British Perspectives on Terrorism*. Boston: George Allen & Unwin. A look at the history of terrorism in Britain and the government's response to this phenomenon, largely attributed to the IRA or the PIRA. The author also makes some suggestions on how to combat terrorism. Chief among these suggestions is increased cooperation between nations and a more effective framework of international law to deal with terrorism. He also recommends a strict policy of non-negotiation with terrorists and that an international antiterrorist body be formed to help in assessing and dealing with terrorist threats as well as an international organization that will minister to the needs of victims of international terrorism.